THE FEMALE MAN

JOANNA RUSS

THE FEMALE MAN

Beacon Press   Boston

Beacon Press
25 Beacon Street
Boston, Massachusetts 02108

Beacon Press books are published under the auspices
of the Unitarian Universalist Association
of Congregations in North America.

Printed in the United States of America

92 91   8 7 6 5

Library of Congress Cataloging-in-Publication Data

Russ, Joanna, 1937–
The female man.

I. Title.
[PS3568.U763F4 1986]   813 .54   86-47511
ISBN 0-8070-6313-4 (pbk.)

This book is dedicated to Anne, to Mary and to the other one and three-quarters billions of us.

If Jack succeeds in forgetting something, this is of little use if Jill continues to remind him of it. He must induce her not to do so. The safest way would be not just to make her keep quiet about it, but to induce her to forget it also.

Jack may act upon Jill in many ways. He may make her feel guilty for keeping on "bringing it up." He may *invalidate* her experience. This can be done more or less radically. He can indicate merely that it is unimportant or trivial, whereas it is important and significant to her. Going further, he can shift the *modality* of her experience from memory to imagination: "It's all in your imagination." Further still, he can invalidate the *content:* "It never happened that way." Finally, he can invalidate not only the significance, modality, and content, but her very capacity to remember at all, and make her feel guilty for doing so into the bargain.

This is not unusual. People are doing such things to each other all the time. In order for such transpersonal invalidation to work, however, it is advisable to overlay it with a thick patina of mystification. For instance, by denying that this is what one is doing, and further invalidating any perception that it is being done by ascriptions such as "How can you think such a thing?" "You must be paranoid." And so on.

R. D. Laing, *The Politics of Experience*, Penguin Books, Ltd., London, 1967, pp. 31-32.

PART ONE

I

I was born on a farm on Whileaway. When I was five I was sent to a school on South Continent (like everybody else) and when I turned twelve I rejoined my family. My mother's name was Eva, my other mother's name Alicia; I am Janet Evason. When I was thirteen I stalked and killed a wolf, alone, on North Continent above the forty-eighth parallel, using only a rifle. I made a travois for the head and paws, then abandoned the head, and finally got home with one paw, proof enough (I thought). I've worked in the mines, on the radio network, on a milk farm, a vegetable farm, and for six weeks as a librarian after I broke my leg. At thirty I bore Yuriko Janetson; when she was taken away to a school five years later (and I never saw a child protest so much) I decided to take time off and see if I could find my family's old home—for they had moved away after I had married and relocated near Mine City in South Continent. The place was unrecognizable, however; our rural areas are always changing. I could find nothing but the tripods of the computer beacons everywhere, some strange crops in the fields that I had never seen before, and a band of wandering children. They were heading North to visit the polar station and offered to lend me a sleeping bag for the night, but I declined and stayed with the resident family; in the morning I started home. Since then I have been Safety Officer for the county, that is S & P (Safety and Peace), a position I have held now for six years. My Stanford-Binet corrected score (in your terms) is 187, my wife's 205 and my daughter's 193. Yuki goes through the ceiling on the verbal test. I've supervised the digging of fire trails, delivered babies, fixed machinery, and milked more moo-cows than I wish I knew existed. But Yuki is crazy about ice-cream. I love my daughter. I love my family (there are nineteen of us). I love my wife (Vittoria). I've fought four duels. I've killed four times.

II

Jeannine Dadier (DADE-yer) worked as a librarian in New York City three days a week for the W.P.A. She worked at the Tompkins Square Branch in the Young Adult section. She wondered sometimes if it was so lucky that Herr Shicklgruber had died in 1936 (the library had books about this). On the third Monday in March of 1969 she saw the first headlines about Janet Evason but paid no attention to them; she spent the day stamping Out books for the Young Adults and checking the lines around her eyes in her pocket mirror (*I'm only twenty-nine!*). Twice she had had to tuck her skirt above her knees and climb the ladder to the higher-up books; once she had to move the ladder over Mrs. Allison and the new gentleman assistant, who were standing below soberly discussing the possibility of war with Japan. There was an article in *The Saturday Evening Post*.

"I don't believe it," said Jeannine Nancy Dadier softly. Mrs. Allison was a Negro. It was an unusually warm, hazy day with a little green showing in the park: imaginary green, perhaps, as if the world had taken an odd turning and were bowling down Spring in a dim bye-street somewhere, clouds of imagination around the trees.

"I don't believe it," repeated Jeannine Dadier, not knowing what they were talking about. "You'd better

2

believe it!" said Mrs. Allison sharply. Jeannine balanced on one foot. (Nice girls don't do that.) She climbed down the ladder with her books and put them on the reserve table. Mrs. Allison didn't like W.P.A. girls. Jeannine saw the headlines again, on Mrs. Allison's newspaper.

WOMAN APPEARS FROM NOWHERE ON
BROADWAY, POLICEMAN VANISHES

"I don't—" (*I have my cat, I have my room, I have my hot plate and my window and the ailanthus tree.*)

Out of the corner of her eye she saw Cal outside in the street; he was walking bouncily and his hat was tipped forward; he was going to have some silly thing or other to say about being a reporter, little blond hatchet face and serious blue eyes; "I'll make it some day, baby." Jeannine slipped into the stacks, hiding behind Mrs. Allison's *P.M.-Post:* Woman Appears from Nowhere on Broadway, Policeman Vanishes. She daydreamed about buying fruit at the free market, though her hands always sweated so when she bought things outside the government store and she couldn't bargain. She would get cat food and feed Mr. Frosty the first thing she got to her room; he ate out of an old china saucer. Jeannine imagined Mr. Frosty rubbing against her legs, his tail waving. Mr. Frosty was marked black-and-white all over. With her eyes closed, Jeannine saw him jump up on the mantelpiece and walk among her things: her sea shells and miniatures. "No, no, *no!*" she said. The cat jumped off, knocking over one of her Japanese dolls. After dinner Jeannine took him out; then she washed the dishes and tried to mend some of her old clothing. She'd go over the ration books. When it got dark she'd turn on the radio for the evening program or she'd read, maybe call up from the drugstore and find out about the boarding house in New Jersey. She might call her brother. She would certainly plant the orange seeds and water them. She thought of Mr. Frosty stalking a bath-robe tail among the miniature orange trees; he'd look like a tiger. If she could get empty cans at the government store.

"Hey, baby?" It was a horrid shock. It was Cal.

3

"No," said Jeannine hastily. "I haven't got time."

"Baby?" He was pulling her arm. Come for a cup of coffee. But she couldn't. She had to learn Greek (the book was in the reserve desk). There was too much to do. He was frowning and pleading. She could feel the pillow under her back already, and Mr. Frosty stalking around them, looking at her with his strange blue eyes, walking widdershins around the lovers. He was part Siamese; Cal called him The Blotchy Skinny Cat. Cal always wanted to do experiments with him, dropping him from the back of a chair, putting things in his way, hiding from him. Mr. Frosty just spat at him now.

"Later," said Jeannine desperately. Cal leaned over her and whispered into her ear; it made her want to cry. He rocked back and forth on his heels. Then he said, "I'll wait." He sat on Jeannine's stack chair, picking up the newspaper, and added:

"The vanishing woman. That's you." She closed her eyes and daydreamed about Mr. Frosty curled up on the mantel, peacefully asleep, all felinity in one circle. Such a spoiled cat.

"Baby?" said Cal.

"Oh, all right," said Jeannine hopelessly, "all right."

I'll watch the ailanthus tree.

III

Janet Evason appeared on Broadway at two o'clock in the afternoon in her underwear. She didn't lose her head. Though the nerves try to keep going in the previous track, she went into evasive position the second after she arrived (good for her) with her fair, dirty hair flying and her khaki shorts and shirt stained with sweat. When a policeman tried to take her arm, she threatened him with le savate, but he vanished. She seemed to regard the crowds around her with a special horror. The policeman reappeared in the same spot an hour later with no memory of the interval, but Janet

4

Evason had returned to her sleeping bag in the New Forest only a few moments after her arrival. A few words of Pan-Russian and she was gone. The last of them waked her bedmate in the New Forest.

"Go to sleep," said the anonymous friend-for-the-night, a nose, a brow, and a coil of dark hair in the dappled moonlight.

"But who has been mucking about with my head!" said Janet Evason.

IV

When Janet Evason returned to the New Forest and the experimenters at the Pole Station were laughing their heads off (for it was not a dream) I sat in a cocktail party in mid-Manhattan. I had just changed into a man, me, Joanna. I mean a female man, of course; my body and soul were exactly the same.

So there's me also.

V

The first man to set foot on Whileaway appeared in a field of turnips on North Continent. He was wearing a blue suit like a hiker's and a blue cap. The farm people had been notified. One, seeing the blip on the tractor's infrared scan, came to get him; the man in blue saw a flying machine with no wings but a skirt of dust and air. The county's repair shed for farm machinery was nearby that week, so the tractor-driver led him there; he was not saying anything intelligible. He saw a translucent dome, the surface undulating slightly. There was an exhaust fan set in one side. Within the dome was a wilderness of machines: dead, on their sides, some turned inside out, their guts spilling on to the grass. From an extended framework under the roof swung hands as big as three men. One of these picked up a car and dropped it. The sides of the car fell off. Littler hands sprang up from the grass.

"Hey, hey!" said the tractor-driver, knocking on a solid piece set into the wall. "It fell, it passed out!"

"Send it back," said an operator, climbing out from under the induction helmet at the far end of the shed. Four others came and stood around the man in the blue suit.

"Is he of steady mind?" said one.

"We don't know."

"Is he ill?"

"Hypnotize him and send him back."

The man in blue—if he had seen them—would have found them very odd: smooth-faced, smooth-skinned, too small and too plump, their coveralls heavy in the seat. They wore coveralls because you couldn't always fix things with the mechanical hands; sometimes you had to use your own. One was old and had white hair; one was very young; one wore the long hair sometimes affected by the youth of Whileaway, "to while away the time." Six pairs of steady curious eyes studied the man in the blue suit.

"That, *mes enfants*," said the tractor-driver at last, "is a man.

"That is a real Earth man."

VI

Sometimes you bend down to tie your shoe, and then you either tie your shoe or you don't; you either straighten up instantly or maybe you don't. Every choice begets at least two worlds of possibility, that is, one in which you do and one in which you don't; or very likely many more, one in which you do quickly, one in which you do slowly, one in which you don't, but hesitate, one in which you hesitate and frown, one in which you hesitate and sneeze, and so on. To carry this line of argument further, there must be an infinite

6

number of possible universes (such is the fecundity of God) for there is no reason to imagine Nature as prejudiced in favor of human action. Every displacement of every molecule, every change in orbit of every electron, every quantum of light that strikes here and not there—each of these must somewhere have its alternative. It's possible, too, that there is no such thing as one clear line or strand of probability, and that we live on a sort of twisted braid, blurring from one to the other without even knowing it, as long as we keep within the limits of a set of variations that really make no difference to us. Thus the paradox of time travel ceases to exist, for the Past one visits is never one's own Past but always somebody else's; or rather, one's visit to the Past instantly creates another Present (one in which the visit has already happened) and what you visit is the Past belonging to that Present—an entirely different matter from your own Past. And with each decision you make (back there in the Past) that new probable universe itself branches, creating simultaneously a new Past and a new Present, or to put it plainly, a new universe. And when you come back to your own Present, you alone know what the other Past was like and what you did there.

Thus it is probable what Whileaway—a name for the Earth ten centuries from now, but not *our* Earth, if you follow me—will find itself not at all affected by this sortie into somebody else's past. And vice versa, of course. The two might as well be independent worlds.

Whileaway, you may gather, is in the future.

But not *our* future.

VII

I saw Jeannine shortly afterward, in a cocktail lounge where I had gone to watch Janet Evason on television (I don't have a set). Jeannine looked very much out of place; I sat next to her and she confided in me: "I don't belong here." I can't imagine how she got

7

there, except by accident. She looked as if she were dressed up for a costume film, sitting in the shadow with her snood and her wedgies, a long-limbed, coltish girl in clothes a little too small for her. Fashion (it seems) is recovering very leisurely from the Great Depression. Not here and now, of course. "I don't belong here!" whispered Jeannine Dadier again, rather anxiously. She was fidgeting. She said, "I don't *like* places like this." She poked the red, tufted leather on the seat.

"What?" I said.

"I went hiking last vacation," she said big-eyed. "That's what I like. It's healthy."

I know it's supposed to be virtuous to run healthily through fields of flowers, but I like bars, hotels, air-conditioning, good restaurants, and jet transport, and I told her so.

"Jet?" she said.

Janet Evason came on the television. It was only a still picture. Then we had the news from Cambodia, Laos, Michigan State, Lake Canandaigua (pollution), and the spinning globe of the world in full color with its seventeen man-made satellites going around it. The color was awful. I've been inside a television studio before: the gallery running around the sides of the barn, every inch of the roof covered with lights, so that the little woman-child with the wee voice can pout over an oven or a sink. Then Janet Evason came on with that blobby look people have on the tube. She moved carefully and looked at everything with interest. She was well dressed (in a suit). The host or M.C. or whatever-you-call-him shook hands with her and then everybody shook hands with everybody else, like a French wedding or an early silent movie. *He* was dressed in a suit. Someone guided her to a seat and she smiled and nodded in the exaggerated way you do when you're not sure of doing the right thing. She looked around and shaded her eyes against the lights. Then she spoke.

(The first thing said by the second man ever to visit Whileaway was, "Where are all the men?" Janet Evason, appearing in the Pentagon, hands in her pockets, feet planted far apart, said, "Where the dickens are all the women?")

8

The sound in the television set conked out for a moment and then Jeannine Dadier was gone; she didn't disappear, she just wasn't there any more. Janet Evason got up, shook hands again, looked around her, questioned with her eyes, pantomimed comprehension, nodded, and walked out of camera range. They never did show you the government guards.

I heard it another time and this is how it went:

MC: How do you like it here, Miss Evason?
JE (looks around the studio, confused): It's too hot.
MC: I mean how do you like it on—well, on Earth?
JE: But I live on the earth. (Her attention is a little strained here.)
MC: Perhaps you had better explain what you mean by that—I mean the existence of different probabilities and so on—you were talking about that before.
JE: It's in the newspapers.
MC: But Miss Evason, if you could, please explain it for the people who are watching the program.
JE: Let them read. Can't they read?
(There was a moment's silence. Then the M.C. spoke.)
MC: Our social scientists as well as our physicists tell us they've had to revise a great deal of theory in light of the information brought by our fair visitor from another world. There have been no men on Whileaway for at least eight centuries—I don't mean no human beings, of course, but no men—and this society, run entirely by women, has naturally attracted a great deal of attention since the appearance last week of its representative and its first ambassador, the lady on my left here. Janet Evason, can you tell us how you think your society on Whileaway will react to the reappearance of men from Earth—I mean our present-day Earth, of course—after an isolation of eight hundred years?
JE (She jumped at this one; probably because it was the first question she could understand): Nine hundred years. What men?
MC: What men? Surely you expect men from our society to visit Whileaway.
JE: Why?

9

MC: For information, trade, ah—cultural contact, surely. (laughter) I'm afraid you're making it rather difficult for me, Miss Evason. When the—ah—the plague you spoke of killed the men on Whileaway, weren't they missed? Weren't families broken up? Didn't the whole pattern of life change?

JE (slowly): I suppose people always miss what they are used to. Yes, they were missed. Even a whole set of words, like "he," "man" and so on—these are banned. Then the second generation, they use them to be daring, among themselves, and the third generation doesn't, to be polite, and by the fourth, who cares? Who remembers?

MC: But surely—that is—

JE: Excuse me, perhaps I'm mistaking what you intend to say as this language we're speaking is only a hobby of mine, I am not as fluent as I would wish. What we speak is a pan-Russian even the Russians would not understand; it would be like Middle English to you, only vice-versa.

MC: I see. But to get back to the question—

JE: Yes.

MC (A hard position to be in, between the authorities and this strange personage who is wrapped in ignorance like a savage chief: expressionless, attentive, possibly civilized, completely unknowing. He finally said): Don't you want men to return to Whileaway, Miss Evason?

JE: Why?

MC: One sex is half a species, Miss Evason. I am quoting (and he cited a famous anthropologist). Do you want to banish sex from Whileaway?

JE (with massive dignity and complete naturalness): Huh?

MC: I said: Do you want to banish sex from Whileaway? Sex, family, love, erotic attraction—call it what you like—we all know that your people are competent and intelligent individuals, but do you think that's enough? Surely you have the intellectual knowledge of biology in other species to know what I'm talking about.

JE: I'm married. I have two children. What the devil do you mean?

10

MC: I—Miss Evason—we—well, we know you form what you call marriages, Miss Evason, that you reckon the descent of your children through both partners and that you even have "tribes"—I'm calling them what Sir ———— calls them; I know the translation isn't perfect—and we know that these marriages or tribes form very good institutions for the economic support of the children and for some sort of genetic mixing, though I confess you're way beyond us in the biological sciences. But, Miss Evason, I am not talking about economic institutions or even affectionate ones. Of course the mothers of Whileaway love their children; nobody doubts that. And of course they have affection for each other; nobody doubts that, either. But there is more, much, much more—I am talking about sexual love.

JE (enlightened): Oh! You mean copulation.

MC: Yes.

JE: And you say we don't have that?

MC: Yes.

JE: How foolish of you. Of course we do.

MC: Ah? (He wants to say, "Don't tell me.")

JE: With each other. Allow me to explain.

She was cut off instantly by a commercial poetically describing the joys of unsliced bread. They shrugged (out of camera range). It wouldn't even have gotten that far if Janet had not insisted on attaching a touch-me-not to the replay system. It was a live broadcast, four seconds' lag. I begin to like her more and more. She said, "If you expect me to observe your taboos, I think you will have to be more precise as to exactly what they are." In Jeannine Dadier's world, she was (would be) asked by a lady commentator:

How do the women of Whileaway do their hair?

JE: They hack it off with clam shells.

11

VIII

"Humanity is unnatural!" exclaimed the philosopher Dunyasha Bernadetteson (A.C. 344–426) who suffered all her life from the slip of a genetic surgeon's hand which had given her one mother's jaw and the other mother's teeth—orthodontia is hardly ever necessary on Whileaway. Her daughter's teeth, however, were perfect. Plague came to Whileaway in P.C. 17 (Preceding Catastrophe) and ended in A.C. 03, with half the population dead; it had started so slowly that no one knew about it until it was too late. It attacked males only. Earth had been completely re-formed during the Golden Age (P.C. 300–ca. P.C. 180) and natural conditions presented considerably less difficulty than they might have during a similar catastrophe a millennium or so earlier. At the time of The Despair (as it was popularly called), Whileaway had two continents, called simply North and South Continents, and a great many ideal bays or anchorages in the coastline. Severe climatic conditions did not prevail below 72° S and 68° N latitude. Conventional water traffic, at the time of the Catastrophe, was employed almost exclusively for freight, passenger traffic using the smaller and more flexibly routed hovercraft. Houses were self-contained, with portable power sources, fuel-alcohol motors or solar cells replacing the earlier centralized power. The later invention of practical matter-antimatter reactors (K. Ansky, A.C. 239) produced great optimism for a decade or so, but these devices proved to be too bulky for private use. Katharina Lucyson Ansky (A.C. 201–282) was also responsible for the principles that made genetic surgery possible. (The merging of ova had been practiced for the previous century and a half.) Animal life had become so scarce before the Golden Age that many species were re-invented by enthusiasts of the Ansky Period; in A.C. 280 there was an outbreak of coneys in Newland (an island off the neck of North Continent), a pandemic not without historical precedent. By A.C. 492, through the brilliant agitation of the great Betty Bettinason Murano (A.C. 453–A.C. 502) Terran colonies were re-established on Mars, Ganymede, and in the Asteroids, the Selenic League assisting according to the Treaty of Mare Tenebrum (A.C. 240). Asked what she expected to find in space, Betty Murano made the immortal quip, "Nothing." By the third century A.C. intelligence was a controllable, heritable factor, though aptitudes and interests continued to elude the surgeons and intelligence itself could be raised only grossly. By the fifth century, clan organization had reached its present complex state and the re-cycling of phosphorus was almost completely successful; by the seventh century Jovian mining made it possible to replace a largely glass-and-ceramics technology with some metals (which were also re-cycled) and for the third time in four hundred years (fashions are sometimes cyclic too) duelling became a serious social nuisance. Several local Guilds Councils voted that a successful duellist must undergo the penalty of an accidental murderer and bear a child to replace the life lost, but the solution was too simple-minded to become popular. There was the age of both parties to consider, for example. By the beginning of the ninth century A.C. the induction helmet was a practical possibility, industry was being drastically altered, and the Selenic League had finally outproduced South Continent in kg protein/person/annum. In 913 A.C. an obscure and discontented descendant of Katy Ansky put together various items of mathematical knowledge and thus discovered—or invented—probability mechanics.

In the time of Jesus of Nazareth, dear reader, there were no motor-cars. I still walk, though, sometimes.

That is, a prudent ecologist makes things work as nearly perfectly as they can by themselves, but you also keep the kerosene lantern in the barn just in case, and usually a debate about keeping a horse ends up with the decision that it's too much trouble, so you let the horse go; but the Conservation Point at La Jolla keeps horses. We wouldn't recognize them. The induction hel-

13

met makes it possible for one workwoman to have not only the brute force but also the flexibility and control of thousands; it's turning Whileawayan industry upside down. Most people walk on Whileaway (of course, their feet are perfect). They make haste in odd ways sometimes. In the early days it was enough just to keep alive and keep the children coming. Now they say "When the re-industrialization's complete," and they still walk. Maybe they like it. Probability mechanics offers the possibility—by looping into another continuum, exactly chosen—of teleportation. Chilia Ysayeson Belin lives in Italian ruins (I think this is part of the Vittore Emmanuele monument, though I don't know how it got to Newland) and she's sentimental about it; how can one add indoor plumbing discreetly without an unconscionable amount of work? Her mother, Ysaye, lives in a cave (the Ysaye who put together the theory of probability mechanics). Pre-fabs take only two days to get and no time at all to set up. There are eighteen Belins and twenty-three Moujkis (Ysaye's family; I stayed with both). Whileaway doesn't have true cities. And of course, the tail of a culture is several centuries behind the head. Whileaway is so pastoral that at times one wonders whether the ultimate sophistication may not take us all back to a kind of pre-Paleolithic dawn age, a garden without any artifacts except for what we would call miracles. A Moujki invented non-disposable food containers in her spare time in A.C. 904 because the idea fascinated her; people have been killed for less.

Meanwhile, the ecological housekeeping is enormous.

IX

JE: I bore my child at thirty; we all do. It's a vacation. Almost five years. The baby rooms are full of people reading, painting, singing, as much as they can, to the children, with the children, over the children. ... Like

14

the ancient Chinese custom of the three-years' mourning, an hiatus at just the right time. There has been no leisure at all before and there will be so little after— anything I do, you understand, I mean really do—I must ground thoroughly in those five years. One works with feverish haste. . . . At sixty I will get a sedentary job and have some time for myself again.

COMMENTATOR: And this is considered enough, in Whileaway?

JE: My God, no.

X

Jeannine dawdles. She always hates to get out of bed. She would lie on her side and look at the ailanthus tree until her back began to ache; then she would turn over, hidden in the veils of the leaves, and fall asleep. Tag-ends of dreams till she lay in bed like a puddle and the cat would climb over her. On workdays Jeannine got up early in a kind of waking nightmare: feeling horrid, stumbling to the hall bathroom with sleep all over her. Coffee made her sick. She couldn't sit in the armchair, or drop her slippers, or bend, or lean, or lie down. Mr. Frosty, perambulating on the window sill, walked back and forth in front of the ailanthus tree: Tiger on Frond. The museum. The zoo. The bus to Chinatown. Jeannine sank into the tree gracefully, like a mermaid, bearing with her a tea-cosy to give to the young man who had a huge muffin trembling over his collar where his face ought to have been. Trembling with emotion.

The cat spoke.

She jerked awake. *I'll feed you, Mr. Frosty.*

Mrrrr.

Cal couldn't afford to take her anywhere, really. She had been traveling on the public buses so long that she knew all the routes. Yawning horribly, she ran the water into Mr. Frosty's cat food and put the dish on the floor. He ate in a dignified way; she remembered

how when she had taken him to her brother's, they had
fed him a real raw fish, just caught in the pond by one
of the boys, and how Mr. Frosty had pounced on it,
bolting it, he was so eager. They really do like fish.
Now he played with the saucer, batting it from side to
side, even though he was grown up. Cats were really
much happier after you . . . after you . . . (she yawned)
Oh, it was Chinese Festival Day.

*If I had the money, if I could get my hair done.
. . . He comes into the library; he's a college professor;
no, he's a playboy. "Who's that girl?" Talks to Mrs.
Allison, slyly flattering her. "This is Jeannine." She
casts her eyes down, rich in feminine power. Had my
nails done today. And these are good clothes, they have
taste, my own individuality, my beauty. "There's something about her," he says. "Will you go out with me?"
Later on the roof garden, drinking champagne, "Jeannine, will you—"*

Mr. Frosty, unsatisfied and jealous, puts his claw
into her leg. "All right!" she says, choking on the sound
of her own voice. *Get dressed quick.*

I do (thought Jeannine, looking in the precious
full-length mirror inexplicably left by the previous tenant
on the back of the closet door) *I do look a little bit like
. . . if I tilt my face. Oh! Cal will be SO—MAD—* and
flying back to the bed, she strips off her pajamas and
snatches at the underwear she always leaves out on the
bureau the night before. Jeannine the Water Nymph. *I
dreamed about a young man somewhere.* She doesn't
quite believe in cards or omens, that's totally idiotic,
but sometimes she giggles and thinks it would be nice.
I have big eyes. You are going to meet a tall, dark—

Placing Mr. Frosty firmly on the bed, she pulls
on her sweater and skirt, then brushes her hair, counting strokes under her breath. Her coat is so old. Just a
little bit of make-up, lip pomade and powder. (She for-
got again and got powder on her coat.) If she got out
early, she wouldn't have to meet Cal in the room; he
would play with the cat (down on his hands and knees)
and then want to Make Love; this way's better. The
bus to Chinatown. She stumbled down the stairs in her
haste, catching at the banister. Little Miss Spry, the old

16

lady on the bottom floor, opened her door just in time to catch Miss Dadier flying through the hall. Jeannine saw a small, wrinkled, worried, old face, wispy white hair, and a body like a flour sack done up in a black shapeless dress. One spotted, veined hand round the edge of the door.

"How do, Jeannine. Going out?"

Doubling up in a fit of hysterics, Miss Dadier escaped. *Ooh! To look like that!*

There was Cal, passing the bus station.

XI

Etsuko Belin, stretched cruciform on a glider, shifted her weight and went into a slow turn, seeing fifteen hundred feet below her the rising sun of Whileaway reflected in the glacial-scaur lakes of Mount Strom. She flipped the glider over, and sailing on her back, passed a hawk.

XII

Six months ago at the Chinese New Year, Jeannine had stood in the cold, holding her mittens over her ears to keep out the awful sound of firecrackers. Cal, next to her, watched the dragon dance around in the street.

XIII

I met Janet Evason on Broadway, standing to the side of the parade given in her honor (I was). She leaned out of the limousine and beckoned me in. Surrounded by Secret Service agents. "That one," she said.

Eventually we will all come together.

XIV

Jeannine, out of place, puts her hands over her ears and shuts her eyes on a farm on Whileaway, sitting at the trestle-table under the trees where everybody is eating. *I'm not here. I'm not here.* Chilia Ysayeson's youngest has taken a fancy to the newcomer; Jeannine sees big eyes, big breasts, big shoulders, thick lips, all that grossness. Mr. Frosty is being spoilt, petted and fed by eighteen Belins. *I'm not here.*

XV

JE: Evason is not "son" but "daughter." This is *your* translation.

XVI

And here we are.

PART TWO

I

Who am I?

I know who I am, but what's my brand name?

Me with a new face, a puffy mask. Laid over the old one in strips of plastic, a blond Hallowe'en ghoul on top of the S.S. uniform. I was skinny as a beanpole underneath except for the hands, which were similarly treated, and that very impressive face. I did this once in my line of business, which I'll go into later, and scared the idealistic children who lived downstairs. Their delicate skins red with offended horror. Their clear young voices raised in song (at three in the morning). I'm not Jeannine. I'm not Janet. I'm not Joanna.

I don't do this often (say I, the ghoul) but it's great elevator technique, holding your forefinger to the back of somebody's neck while passing the fourth floor, knowing he'll never find out that you're not all there.

(Sorry, But watch out.)

You'll meet me later.

II

As I have said before, I (not the one above, please) had an experience on the seventh of February last, nineteen-sixty-nine.

I turned into a man.

I had been a man before, but only briefly and in a crowd.

You would not have noticed anything, had you been there.

Manhood, children, is not reached by courage or short hair or insensibility or by being (as I was) in Chicago's only skyscraper hotel while the snow rages outside. I sat in a Los Angeles cocktail party with the bad baroque furniture all around, having turned into a man. I saw myself between the dirty-white scrolls of the mirror and the results were indubitable: I was a man. But what then is manhood?

Manhood, children . . . *is Manhood.*

III

Janet beckoned me into the limousine and I got in. The road was very dark. As she opened the door I saw her famous face under the dome light over the front seat; trees massed electric-green beyond the headlights. This is how I really met her. Jeannine Dadier was an evasive outline in the back seat.

"Greetings," said Janet Evason. "Hello. Bonsoir. That's Jeannine. And you?"

I told her. Jeannine started talking about all the clever things her cat had done. Trees swayed and jerked in front of us.

"On moonlit nights," said Janet, "I often drive without lights," and slowing the car to a crawl, she turned out the headlights; I mean I saw them disappear—the countryside blent misty and pale to the horizon like a badly exposed Watteau. I always feel in moonlight as though my eyes have gone bad. The car—something expensive, though it was too dark to tell what—sighed soundlessly. Jeannine had all but disappeared.

"I have, as they say," (said Janet in her surprisingly loud, normal voice) "given them the slip," and she turned the headlights back on. "I daresay that's not proper," she added.

"It is *not*," said Jeannine from the back seat. We passed a motel sign in a dip of the road, with something flashing lit-up behind the trees.

"I am very sorry," said Janet. *The car?* "Stolen," she said. She peered out the side window for a moment, turning her head and taking her eyes off the road. Jeannine gasped indignantly. Only the driver can see really accurately in the rear-view mirror; but there was a car behind us. We turned off onto a dirt road—that is, she turned off—and into the woods with the headlights dark—and on to another road, after which there was a private house, all lights out, just as neat as you please. "Goodbye, excuse me," said Janet affably, slipping out of the car; "Carry on, please," and she vanished into the house. She was wearing her television suit. I sat baffled, with Jeannine's hands gripping the car seat at my back (the way children do). The second car pulled up behind us. They came out and surrounded me (such a disadvantage to be sitting down and the lights hurt your eyes). Brutally short haircuts and something unpleasant about the clothing: straight, square, clean, yet not robust. Can you picture a plainclothesman pulling his hair? Of course not. Jeannine was cowering out of sight or had disappeared somehow. Just before Janet Evason emerged on to the porch of that private house, accompanied by a beaming family: father, mother, teen-age daughter, and family dog (everyone delighted to be famous), I committed myself rather too idiotically by exclaiming with some heat:

"Who are you looking for? There's nobody here. There's only me."

IV

Was she trying to run away? Or only to pick people at random?

21

V

Why did they send me? Because they can spare me. Etsuko Belin strapped me in. "Ah, Janet!" she said. (Ah, yourself.) In a plain, blank room. The cage in which I lay goes in and out of existence forty-thousand times a second; thus it did not go with me. No last kiss from Vittoria; nobody could get to me. I did not, contrary to your expectation, go nauseated or cold or feel I was dropping through endless whatever. The trouble is your brain continues to work on the old stimuli while the new ones already come in; I tried to *make* the new wall into the old. Where the lattice of the cage had been was a human face.

Späsibo.

Sorry.

Let me explain.

I was so rattled that I did not take in all at once that I was lying across her—desk, I learned later—and worse still. Appeared across it, just like that (in full view of five others). We had experimented with other distances; now they fetched me back, to make sure, and sent me out, and there I was again, on her desk.

What a strange woman; thick and thin, dried up, hefty in the back, with a grandmotherly moustache, a little one. How withered away one can be from a life of unremitting toil.

Aha! A man.

Shall I say my flesh crawled? Bad for vanity, but it did. This must be a man. I got off its desk. Perhaps it was going out to manual work, for we were dressed alike; only it had coded bands of color sewn over its pocket, a sensible device for a machine to read or something. I said in perfect English:

"How do you do? I must explain my sudden appearance. I am from another time." (We had rejected *probability/continuum* as unintelligible.) Nobody moved.

22

"How do you do? I must explain my sudden appearance. I am from another time."

What do you do, call them names? They didn't move. I sat down on the desk and one of them slammed shut a part of the wall; so they have doors, just as we do. The important thing in a new situation is not to frighten, and in my pockets was just the thing for such an emergency. I took out the piece of string and began playing Cat's Cradle.

"Who are you!" said one of them. They all had these little stripes over their pockets.

"I am from another time, from the future," I said, and held out the cat's cradle. It's not only the universal symbol of peace, but a pretty good game, too. This was the simplest position, though. One of them laughed; another put its hands over its eyes; the one whose desk it was backed off; a fourth said, "Is this a joke?"

"I am from the future." Just sit there long enough and the truth will sink in.

"What?" said Number One.

"How else do you think I appeared out of the air?" I said. "People cannot very well walk through walls, now can they?"

The reply to this was that Three took out a small revolver, and this surprised me; for everyone knows that anger is most intense towards those you know: it is lovers and neighbors who kill each other. There's no sense, after all, in behaving that way towards a perfect stranger; where's the satisfaction? No love, no need; no need, no frustration; no frustration, no hate, right? It must have been fear. The door opened at this point and a young woman walked in, a woman of thirty years or so, elaborately painted and dressed. I know I should not have assumed anything, but one must work with what one has; and I assumed that her dress indicated a mother. That is, someone on vacation, someone with leisure, someone who's close to the information network and full of intellectual curiosity. If there's a top class (I said to myself), this is it. I didn't want to take anyone away from necessary manual work. And I thought, you know, that I would make a small joke. So I said to her:

"Take me to your leader."

23

VI

   . . . a tall blonde woman in blue pajamas who appeared standing on Colonel Q————'s desk, as if from nowhere. She took out what appeared to be a weapon. . . . No answer to our questions. The Colonel has kept a small revolver in the top drawer of his desk since the summer riots. He produced it. She would not answer our questions. I believe at that point Miss X————, the Colonel's secretary, walked into the room, quite unaware of what was going on. Luckily Y————, Z————, Q————, R————, and myself kept our heads. She then said, "I am from the future."

   QUESTIONER: Miss X———— said that?

   ANSWER: No, not Miss X————. The—the stranger.

   QUESTIONER: Are you sure she appeared *standing* on Colonel Q————'s desk?

   ANSWER: No, I'm not sure. Wait. Yes I am. She was sitting on it.

VII

   INTERVIEWER: It seems odd to all of us, Miss Evason, that in venturing into such—well, such absolutely unknown territory—that you should have come unarmed with anything except a piece of string. Did you expect us to be peaceful?

   JE: No. No one is, completely.

   INTERVIEWER: Then you should have armed yourself.

   JE: Never.

   INTERVIEWER: But an armed person, Miss

Evason, is more formidable than one who is helpless. An armed person more readily inspires fear.

JE: Exactly.

VIII

That woman lived with me for a month. I don't mean in my house. Janet Evason on the radio, the talk shows, the newspapers, newsreels, magazines, ads even. With somebody I suspect was Miss Dadier appearing in my bedroom late one night.

"I'm lost." She meant: what world is this?

"F'godsakes, go out in the *hall*, will you?"

But she melted away through the Chinese print on the wall, presumably into the empty, carpeted, three-in-the-morning corridor outside. Some people never stick around. In my dream somebody wanted to know where Miss Dadier was. I woke at about four and went to the bathroom for a glass of water; there she was on the other side of the bathroom mirror, semaphoring frantically. She made her eyes big and peered desperately into the room, both fists pressed against the glass.

"He's not here," I said. "Go away."

She mouthed something unintelligible. The room sang:

> *Thou hast led capti-*
> *i-vi-ty*
> *Ca-ap-tive!*
>
> *Thous hast led capti-*
> *i-vi-ty*
> *Ca-ap-tive!*

I wet a washcloth and swiped at the mirror with it. She winced. Turn out the light, said my finer instincts, and so I turned out the light. She remained lit up. Dismissing the whole thing as the world's aberration and not mine, I went back to bed.

25

"Janet?" she said.

IX

Janet picked up Jeannine at the Chinese New Festival. Miss Dadier never allowed anyone to pick her up but a woman was different, after all; it wasn't the same thing. Janet was wearing a tan raincoat. Cal had gone round the corner to get steamed buns in a Chinese luncheonette and Miss Evason asked the meaning of a banner that was being carried through the street.

"Happy Perseverance, Madam Chiang," said Jeannine.

Then they chatted about the weather.

"Oh, I couldn't," said Jeannine suddenly. (She put her hands over her ears and made a face.) "But that's different," she said.

Janet Evason made another suggestion. Jeannine looked interested and willing to understand, though a little baffled.

"Cal's in there," said Jeannine loftily. "I couldn't go in *there*." She spread her fingers out in front of her like two fans. She was prettier than Miss Evason and glad of it; Miss Evason resembled a large boy scout with flyaway hair.

"Are you French?"

"Ah!" said Miss Evason, nodding.

"I've never been to France," said Jeannine languidly; "I often thought I'd—well, I just haven't been." *Don't stare at me.* She slouched and narrowed her eyes. She wanted to put one hand up affectedly to shade her forehead; she wanted to cry out, "Look! There's my boyfriend Cal," but there wasn't a sign of him, and if she turned to the grocery-store window it would be full of fish's intestines and slabs of dried fish; she knew that.

It—would—make—her—*sick!* (She stared at a carp with its guts coming out.) *I'm shaking all over.*

26

"Who did your hair?" she asked Miss Evason, and when Miss Evason didn't understand:

"Who streaked your hair so beautifully?"

"Time," and Miss Evason laughed and Miss Dadier laughed. Miss Dadier laughed beautifully, gloriously, throwing her head back; everyone admired the curve of Miss Dadier's throat. Eyes turned. *A beautiful body and personality to burn.* "I can't possibly go with you," said Miss Dadier magnificently, her fur coat swirling; "There's Cal, there's New York, there's my work, New York in springtime, I can't leave, my life is here," and the spring wind played with her hair.

Crazy Jeannine nodded, petrified.

"Good," said Janet Evason. "We'll get you a leave from work." She whistled and around the corner at a dead run came two plainclothes policemen in tan raincoats: enormous, jowly, thick-necked, determined men who will continue running—at a dead heat—through the rest of this tale. But we won't notice them. Jeannine looked in astonishment from their raincoats to Miss Evason's raincoat. She did not approve *at all.*

"So that's why it doesn't fit," she said. Janet pointed to Jeannine for the benefit of the cops.

"Boys, I've got one."

X

The Chinese New Festival was invented to celebrate the recapture of Hong Kong from the Japanese. Chiang Kai-shek died of heart disease in 1951 and Madam Chiang is premieress of the New China. Japan, which controls the mainland, remains fairly quiet since it lacks the backing of—for example—a reawakened Germany, and if any war occurs, it will be between the Divine Japanese Imperiality and the Union of Soviet Socialist Republics (there are twelve). Americans don't worry much. Germany still squabbles occasionally with Italy or England; France (disgraced in the abortive *putsch* of '42) is beginning to have trouble with its

27

colonial possessions. Britain—wiser—gave India provisional self-government in 1966.

The Depression is still world-wide.

(But think—only think!—what might have happened if the world had not so luckily slowed down, if there had been a really big war, for big wars are forcing-houses of science, economics, politics; think what might have happened, what might not have happened. It's a lucky world. Jeannine is lucky to live in it.

She doesn't think so.)

XI

(Cal, who came out of the Chinese luncheonette just in time to see his girl go off with three other people, did not throw the lunch buns to the ground in a fit of exasperated rage and stamp on them. Some haunted Polish ancestor looked out of his eyes. He was so thin and slight that his ambitions shone through him: I'll make it some day, baby. I'll be the greatest. He sat down on a fire plug and began to eat the buns.

(She'll have to come back to feed her cat.)

PART THREE

I

This is the lecture. If you don't like it, you can
skip to the next chapter. Before Janet
arrived on this planet

I was moody, ill-at-ease, unhappy, and hard to be with.
I didn't relish my breakfast. I spent my whole day
combing my hair and putting on make-up. Other girls
practiced with the shot-put and compared archery
scores, but I—indifferent to javelin and crossbow, positively repelled by horticulture and ice hockey—all I did
was

dress for The Man
smile for The Man
talk wittily to The Man
sympathize with The Man
flatter The Man
understand The Man
defer to The Man
entertain The Man
keep The Man
live for The Man.

Then a new interest entered my life. After I called
up Janet, out of nothing, or she called up me (don't
read between the lines; there's nothing there) I began to
gain weight, my appetite improved, friends commented
on my renewed zest for life, and a nagging scoliosis of
the ankle that had tortured me for years simply vanished overnight. I don't even remember the last time I
had to go to the aquarium and stifle my sobs by

watching the sharks. I rode in closed limousines with Janet to television appearances much like the one you already saw in the last chapter; I answered her questions; I bought her a pocket dictionary; I took her to the zoo; I pointed out New York's skyline at night as if I owned it.

Oh, I made that woman up; you can believe it!

Now in the opera scenario that governs our lives, Janet would have gone to a party and at that party she would have met a man and there would have been something about that man; he would not have seemed to her like any other man she had ever met. Later he would have complimented her on her eyes and she would have blushed with pleasure; she would have felt that compliment was somehow unlike any other compliment she had ever received because it had come from that man; she would have wanted to please that man, and at the same time she would have felt the compliment enter the marrow of her bones; she would have gone out and bought mascara for the eyes that had been complimented by that man. And later still they would have gone for walks, and later still for dinners; and little dinners tête-à-tête with that man would have been like no other dinners Janet had ever had; and over the coffee and brandy he would have taken her hand; and later still Janet would have melted back against the black leather couch in his apartment and thrown her arm across the cocktail table (which would have been made of elegant teak-wood) and put down her drink of expensive Scotch and swooned; she would have simply swooned. She would have said: I Am In Love With That Man. That Is The Meaning Of My Life. And then, of course, you know what would have happened.

I made her up. I did everything but find a typical family for her; if you will remember, she found them herself. But I taught her how to use a bath-tub and I corrected her English (calm, slow, a hint of whisper in the "s," guardedly ironic). I took her out of her workingwoman's suit and murmured (as I soaped her hair) fragments of sentences that I could somehow never finish: "Janet you must ... Janet, we don't ... but one always . . ."

That's different, I said, *that's different.*

I couldn't, I said, *oh, I couldn't.*

What I want to say is, I tried; I'm a good girl; I'll do it if you'll show me.

But what can you do when this woman puts her hand through the wall? (Actually the plasterboard partition between the kitchenette and the living room.)

Janet, sit down.

Janet, don't do that.

Janet, don't kick Jeannine.

Janet!

Janet, don't!

I imagine her: civil, reserved, impenetrably formulaic. She was on her company manners for months. Then, I think, she decided that she could get away with having no manners; or rather, that we didn't honor the ones she had, so why not? It must have been new to someone from Whileaway, the official tolerance of everything she did or tried to do, the leisure, the attention that was so close to adulation. I have the feeling that any of them can blossom out like that (and lucky they don't, eh?) with the smooth kinship web of home centuries away, surrounded by barbarians, celibate for months, coping with a culture and a language that I think she—in her heart—must have despised.

I was housed with her for six and a half months in a hotel suite ordinarily used to entertain visiting diplomats. *I put shoes on that woman's feet.* I had fulfilled one of my dreams—to show Manhattan to a foreigner—and I waited for Janet to go to a party and meet that man; I waited and waited. She walked around the suite nude. She has an awfully big ass. She used to practice her yoga on the white living room rug, callouses on her feet actually catching in the fuzz, if you can believe it. I would put lipstick on Janet and ten minutes later it would have vanished; I clothed her and she shed like a three-year-old: courteous, kind, irreproachably polite; I shied at her atrocious jokes and she made them worse.

31

She never communicated with her home, as far as I know.

She wanted to see a man naked (we got pictures).

She wanted to see a baby man naked (we got somebody's nephew).

She wanted newspapers, novels, histories, magazines, people to interview, television programs, statistics on clove production in the East Indies, textbooks on wheat farming, to visit a bridge (we did). She wanted the blueprints (we got them).

She was neat but lazy—I never caught her doing anything.

She held the baby like an expert, cooing and trundling, bouncing him up and down so that he stopped screaming and stared at her chin the way babies do. She uncovered him. "Tsk." "My goodness." She was astonished.

She scrubbed my back and asked me to scrub hers; she took the lipstick I gave her and made pictures on the yellow damask walls. ("You mean it's not *washable?*") I got her girlie magazines and she said she couldn't make head or tail of them; I said, "Janet, stop joking" and she was surprised; she hadn't meant to. She wanted a dictionary of slang. One day I caught her playing games with Room Service; she was calling up the different numbers on the white hotel phone and giving them contradictory instructions. This woman was dialing the numbers with her feet. I slammed the phone across one of the double beds.

"Joanna," she said, "I do not understand you. Why not play? Nobody is going to be hurt and nobody is going to blame you; why not take advantage?"

"You fake!" I said; "You fake, you rotten fake!" Somehow that was all I could think of to say. She tried looking injured and did not succeed—she only looked smug—so she wiped her face clean of all expression and started again.

"If we make perhaps an hypothetical assumption—"

"Go to hell," I said; "Put your clothes on."

"Perhaps about this sex business you can tell me," she said, "why is this hypothetical assumption—"

"Why the devil do you run around in the nude!"

"My child," she said gently, "you must understand. I'm far from home; I want to keep myself cheerful, eh? And about this men thing, you must remember that to me they are a particularly foreign species; one can make love with a dog, yes? But not with something so unfortunately close to oneself. You see how I can feel this way?"

My ruffled dignity. She submitted to the lipstick again. We got her dressed. She looked all right except for that unfortunate habit of whirling around with a grin on her face and her hands out in the judo crouch. Well, well! I got reasonably decent shoes on Janet Evason's feet. She smiled. She put her arm around me.

Oh, I couldn't!

?

That's different.

(You'll hear a lot of those two sentences in life, if you listen for them. I see Janet Evason finally dressing herself, a study in purest awe as she holds up to the light, one after the other, semi-transparent garments of nylon and lace, fairy webs, rose-colored elastic puttees—"Oh, my," "Oh, my goodness," she says—and finally, completely stupefied, wraps one of them around her head.)

She bent down to kiss me, looking kind, looking perplexed, and I kicked her.

That's when she put her fist through the wall.

II

We went to a party on Riverside Drive—incognitae—with Janet a little behind me. At the door, a little behind me. The February snow coming down outside. On the fortieth floor we got out of the elevator and I checked my dress in the hall mirror: my hair feels as if it's falling down, my makeup's too heavy, everything's out of place from the crotch of the panty-hose to the ridden-up bra to the ring whose stone drags it around

33

under my knuckle. And I don't even wear false eye-lashes. Janet—beastly fresh—is showing her usual trick of the Disappearing Lipstick. She hums gently. Batty Joanna. There are policemen posted all around the building, policemen in the street, policemen in the elevator. Nobody wants anything to happen to her. She gives a little yelp of excitement and pleasure—the first uncontrolled contact with the beastly savages.

"You'll tell me what to do," she says, "won't you?" Ha ha. He he. Ho ho. What fun. She bounces up and down.

"Why didn't they send someone who knew what he was doing!" I whisper back.

"What *she* was doing," she says unself-consciously, shifting gears in a moment. "You see, under field conditions, nobody can handle all the eventualities. We're not superhuman, any of us, *nicht wahr?* So you take someone you can spare. It's like this—"

I opened the door, Janet a little behind me.

I knew most of the women there: Sposissa, three times divorced; Eglantissa, who thinks only of clothes; Aphrodissa, who cannot keep her eyes open because of her false eyelashes; Clarissa, who will commit suicide; Lucrissa, whose strained forehead shows that she's making more money than her husband; Wailissa, engaged in a game of ain't-it-awful with Lamentissa; Travailissa, who usually only works, but who is now sitting very still on the couch so that her smile will not spoil; and naughty Saccharissa, who is playing a round of His Little Girl across the bar with the host. Saccharissa is forty-five. So is Amicissa, the Good Sport. I looked for Ludicrissa, but she is too plain to be invited to a party like this, and of course we never invite Amphibissa, for obvious reasons.

In we walked, Janet and I, the right and left hands of a bomb. Actually you might have said everyone was enjoying themselves. I introduced her to everyone. My Swedish cousin. (Where is Domicissa, who never opens her mouth in public? And Dulcississa, whose standard line, "Oh, you're so wonderful!" is oddly missing from the air tonight?)

I shadowed Janet.

I played with my ring.

I waited for the remark that begins "Women—" or "Women can't—" or "Why do women—" and kept up an insubstantial conversation on my right. On my left hand Janet stood: very erect, her eyes shining, turning her head swiftly every now and again to follow the current of events at the party. At times like this, when I'm low, when I'm anxious, Janet's attention seems a parody of attention and her energy unbearably high. I was afraid she'd burst out chuckling. Somebody (male) got me a drink.

A ROUND OF "HIS LITTLE GIRL"

SACCHARISSA: I'm Your Little Girl.
HOST (wheedling): Are you really?
SACCHARISSA (complacent): Yes I am.
HOST: Then you have to be stupid, too.

A SIMULTANEOUS ROUND OF "AIN'T IT AWFUL"

LAMENTISSA: When I do the floor, he doesn't come home and say it's wonderful.
WAILISSA: Well, darling, we can't live without him, can we? You'll just have to do *better*.
LAMENTISSA (wistfully): I bet *you* do better.
WAILISSA: I do the floor better than anybody I know.
LAMENTISSA (excited): Does he ever say it's wonderful?
WAILISSA (dissolving): He never says *anything!*

(There follows the chorus which gives the game its name. A passing male, hearing this exchange, remarked, "You women are lucky you don't have to go out and go to work.")

Somebody I did not know came up to us: sharp, balding, glasses reflecting two spots of lamplight. A long, lean, academic, more-or-less young man.

"Do you want something to drink?"

Janet said "A-a-a-h" very long, with exaggerated enthusiasm. Dear God, don't let her make a fool of herself. "Drink what?" she said promptly. I introduced my Swedish cousin.

"Scotch, punch, rum-and-coke, rum, ginger-ale?"

"What's that?" I suppose that, critically speaking, she didn't look too bad. "I mean," she said (correcting herself), "that is what kind of drug? Excuse me. My English isn't good." She waits, delighted with everything. He smiles.

"Alcohol," he says.

"*Ethyl* alcohol?" She puts her hand over her heart in unconscious parody. "It is made from grain, yes? Food? Potatoes? My, my! How wasteful!"

"Why do you say that?" says the young man, laughing.

"Because," answers my Janet, "to use food for fermentation is wasteful, yes? I should think so! That's cultivation, fertilizer, sprays, harvesting, et cetera. Then you lose a good deal of the carbohydrates in the actual process. I should think you would grow *cannabis,* which my friend tells me you already have, and give the grains to those starving people."

"You know, you're charming," he says.

"Huh?" (That's Janet.) To prevent disaster, I step in and indicate with my eyes that yes, she's charming and second, we really do want a drink.

"You told me you people had cannabis," Janet says a little irritably.

"It isn't cured properly; it'll make you choke," I say. She nods thoughtfully. I can tell without asking what's going through her mind: the orderly fields of Whileaway, the centuries-old mutations and hybridizations of cannabis sativa, the little garden plots of marihuana tended (for all I know) by seven-year-olds. She had in fact tried some several weeks before. It had made her cough horribly.

The youngish man returned with our drink and while I signalled him Stay, stay, she's harmless, she's innocent, Janet screwed up her face and tried to drink the stuff in one swallow. It was then I knew that her sense of humor was running away with her. She turned red. She coughed explosively.

"It's horrible!"

"*Sip* it, *sip* it," said he, highly amused.

"I don't want it."

"I tell you what," he proposed amiably, "I'll make you one you *will* like." (There follows a small interlude of us punching each other and whispering vehemently: "Janet, if you—")

"But I don't like it," she said simply. You're not supposed to do that. On Whileaway, perhaps, but not here.

"Try it," he urged.

"I did," she said equably. "Sorry, I will wait for the smokes."

He takes her hand and closes her fingers around the glass, shaking his forefinger at her playfully: "Come on now, I can't believe that; you made me get it for you—" and as our methods of courtship seem to make her turn pale, I wink at him and whisk her away to the corner of the apartment where the C.S. vapor blooms. She tries it and gets a coughing fit. She goes sullenly back to the bar.

A MANUFACTURER OF CARS FROM LEEDS (genteelly): I hear so much about the New Feminism here in America. Surely it's not necessary, is it? (He beams with the delighted air of someone who has just given pleasure to a whole roomful of people.)

SPOSISSA, EGLANTISSA, APHRODISSA, CLARISSA, LU-CRISSA, WAILISSA, LAMENTISSA, TRAVAILISSA (dear God, how many of them are there?), SACCHARISSA, LUDICRISSA (she came in late): Oh no, no, no! (They all laugh.)

When I got back to the bar, Clarissa was going grimly into her latest heartbreak. I saw Janet, feet apart—a daughter of Whileaway never quails!—trying to get down more than three ounces of straight rum. I suppose one forgets the first taste. She looked flushed and successful.

ME: You're not used to that stuff, Janet.

JANET: O.K., I'll stop.

(Like all foreigners she is fascinated by the word

37

"Okay" and has been using it on every possible occasion for the last four weeks.)

"It's very hard not having anything, though," she says seriously. "I suppose, love, that I'm hardly giving anything away if I say that I don't like your friends."

"They're not my friends, for God's sake. I come here to meet people."

?

"I come here to meet men," I said. "Janet, sit down."

This time it was a ginger moustache. Young. Nice. Flashy. Flowered waistcoat. Hip. (hip?)

Peals of laughter from the corner, where Eglantissa's latest is holding up and wiggling a chain made of paper clips. Wailissa fusses ineffectually around him. Eglantissa—looking more and more like a corpse—sits on an elegant, brocaded armchair, with her drink rigid in her hand. Blue smoke wreathes about her head.

"Hullo," says Ginger Moustache. Sincere. Young.

"Oh. How do you do?" says Janet. She's remembered her manners. Ginger Moustache produces a smile and a cigarette case.

"Marijuana?" says Janet hopefully. He chuckles.

"No. Do you want a drink?"

She looks sulky.

"All right, don't have a drink. And you're—"

I introduce my cousin from Sweden.

"Why do you people catabolize foodstuffs in this way?" she bursts out. Still on her mind, it seems. I explain.

"Sickness," he says. "I'm not an alcohol head; that's not my bag. I agree with you. I'd just as soon see people eating the stuff."

(Amicissa dreams: perhaps he won't have the insatiable vanity, the uneasy aggressiveness, the quickness to resent any slight or fancied neglect. Perhaps he won't want to be top dog all the time. And he won't have a fiancée. And he won't be married. And he won't be gay. And he won't have children. And he won't be sixty.)

"A-a-ah," says Janet, letting out a long breath. "Yes. Aha."

I left them for a while. I was alert to any opportunity. I was graceful. I smiled.

My brassiere hurts.

When I got back they had reached the stage of Discussing His Work. He was teaching high school but was going to be fired. For his ties, I think. Janet was very interested. She mentioned the—uh—day nurseries in—well, in Sweden—and quoted:

"We have a saying: when the child goes to the school, both mother and child howl; the child because it is going to be separated from the mother and the mother because she has to go back to work."

"The tie between mother and child is very important," said Ginger Moustache reprovingly. ("Excuse me, let me move that cushion behind your back.")

"I'm sure Swedish mothers really groove on their kids, though," he added.

"Huh?" said my Janet. (He took it as an ignorance of English and relented.)

"Listen," he said, "some time I want you to meet my wife. I know this is a bad scene—I mean meeting you here with the plastic people, y'know?—but *some day* you're going to come out to Vermont and meet my wife. It's a great, heavy scene. We've got six kids."

"Six you take care of?" said Janet with considerable respect.

"Sure," he said. "They're in Vermont right now. But after this work hassle is over I'm going back. You grok?"

He means do you understand, Janet? She thought it simpler to say yes.

"Hey," said Ginger Moustache, springing to his feet, "it's been great meeting you. You're a real ballsy chick. I mean you're a *woman*."

She looked down at herself. "What?"

"Sorry about the slang; I mean you're a fine person. It's a pleasure—to—know—you."

"You don't know me," she was developing the nasty look. Not very nasty as yet but frustrated-angry, tapping-the-fingers, now-look-here-I-want-this-explained. She is quite spoiled, in her own way.

"Yeah, I know," he said. "How can we get to

39

know each other in ten minutes, huh? That's true. It's a formal phrase: pleasuretoknowyou."

Janet giggled.

"Right?" he said. "Tell you what, give me your name and address." (she gave him mine) "I'll drop you a line. Write a letter, that is." (Not a bad fellow this Ginger Moustache.) He got up and she got up; something must interrupt this idyll. Saccharissa, Ludicrissa, Travailissa, Aphrodissa, Clarissa, Sposissa, Domicissa, the whole gang, even Carissa herself, have formed a solid wall around this couple. Breaths are held. Bets get made. Joanissa is praying in a heap in the corner. Ginger Moustache got up and Janet trailed him into the hall, asking questions. She's a good bit taller than he is. She wants to know about everything. Either she does not mind the lack of sexual interest or—as is more likely in a foreigner—prefers it. Though he's got a wife. The harsh light from the kitchenette strikes Janet Evason's face and there on one side, running from eyebrow to chin, is a strange, fine line. Has she been in an accident?

"Oh, *that*!" says Janet Evason, chuckling, bending over (though somewhat hampered by her party dress), laughing, gasping with little feminine squeaks from the top of the compass right down to the bottom, hoarse and musical, "Oh, *that*!"

"That's from my third duel," she says, "see?" and guides Moustache's hand (his forefinger, actually) along her face.

"Your what?" says Moustache, momentarily frozen into the attractive statue of a pleasant young man.

"My duel," says Janet, "silly. Well, it's not Sweden, not really. You've heard of me; I was on the television. I'm the emissary from Whileaway."

"My God," he says.

"Ssh, don't tell anyone." (She's very pleased with herself. She chuckles.) "*This* line I got in my third duel; *this* one—it's practically gone—in my second. Not bad, hey?"

"Are you sure you don't mean fencing?" says Ginger Moustache.

"Hell, no," says Janet impatiently; "I told you,

40

duel." And she draws her forefinger across her throat with a melodramatic jerk. This mad chick doesn't seem so nice to Moustache any more. He swallows.

"What do you fight about—girls?"

"You are kidding me," says Janet. "We fight about bad temper—what else? Temperamental incompatibility. Not that it's so common as it used to be but if you can't stand her and she can't stand you, what's to be done?"

"Sure," says Ginger Moustache. "Well, goodbye." Janet became suddenly repentant.

"That—well, I suppose that's rather savage, isn't it?" she says. "I beg pardon. You will think badly of us. Understand, I have put all that behind me now; I am an adult; I have a family. We hope to be friends, yes?" And she looks down at him solemnly, a little timidly, ready to be rebuked. But he hasn't the heart to do it.

"You're a great chick," says he. "Some day we'll get together. Don't duel with *me,* though."

She looks surprised. "Huh?"

"Yeah, you'll tell me all about yourself," Ginger Moustache goes on. He smiles and broods. "You can meet the kids."

"I have a daughter," says Janet. "Baby brat Yuriko." He smiles.

"We got homemade wine. Vegetable garden. Sara puts things up. Great place." (He's into his duffle coat by now after searching in the hall closet.) "Tell me, what do you do? I mean for a living?"

"Whileaway is not here-and-now," Janet begins; "You might not understand. I settle family quarrels; I look after people; it's—"

"Social work?" asks Ginger Moustache, extending to us his fine, shapely, tanned, uncalloused hand, an intellectual's hand, but I have hardened my heart and I peep out from behind Janet Evason with the divine relief of my female irony and my female teeth:

"She's a cop. She puts people in jail."

Ginger Moustache is alarmed, knows he's alarmed, laughs at himself, shakes his head. How wide is the gap between cultures! But we grok. We shake hands. He goes off into the party to fetch Domicissa, whom he pulls by the wrist (she silently protesting) to the hall closet. "Get on your Goddamn coat, will you!" I heard only whispers, vehement and angry, then Domicissa blowing her nose.

"So long, hey! Hey, so long!" cried he.

His wife's in Vermont; Domicissa isn't his wife.

Janet had just asked me to explicate the marriage system of North America.

Saccharissa has just said, pouting, "Po' little me! I sho'ly needs to be liberated!"

Aphrodissa was sitting in someone's lap, her left eyelash half off. Janet was rather at a loss. Mustn't judge. Shut one eye. Peek. Busy, busy couple, kissing and grabbing. Janet backed off slowly to the other side of the room and there we met the lean academic with the glasses; he's all sharp, nervous and sharp. He gave her a drink and she drank it.

"So you *do* like it!" he said provokingly.

"I would suhtinly like," said Saccharissa with great energy, "to see all those women athletes from the Olympics compete with all those men athletes; I don't imagine any of these women athletes could even *come neah* the men."

"But American women are so *unusual*," said the man from Leeds. "Your conquering energy, dear lady, all this world-wide American efficiency! What do you dear ladies use it for?"

"Why, to conquer the men!" cried Saccharissa, braying.

"In mah baby brain," said Janet, imitating quite accurately, "a suhtin conviction is beginnin' to fo'm."

"The conviction that somebody is being insulted?" said Sharp Glasses. He didn't say that, actually.

"Let's go," said Janet. *I know it's the wrong party, but where are you going to find the right party?*

"Oh, you don't want to go!" said Sharp Glasses energetically. Jerky, too, they're always so jerky.

"But I do," said Janet.

"Of course you don't," he said; "You're just beginning to enjoy yourself. The party's warming up.

Here," (pushing us down on the couch) "let me get you another."

You're in a strange place, Janet. Be civil.

He came back with another and she drank it. Uh-oh. We made trivial conversation until she recovered. He leaned forward confidentially. "What do *you* think of the new feminism, eh?"

"What is—" (she tried again) "what is—my English is not so good. Could you explain?"

"Well, what do you think of women? Do you think women can compete with men?"

"I don't know any men." She's beginning to get mad.

"Ha ha!" said Sharp Glasses. "Ha ha ha! Ha ha!" (He laughed just like that, in sharp little bursts.) "My name's Ewing. What's yours?"

"Janet."

"Well, Janet, I'll tell you what *I* think of the new feminism. I think it's a mistake. A very bad mistake."

"Oh," said Janet flatly. I kicked her, I kicked her, I kicked her.

"I haven't got anything against women's intelligence," said Ewing. "Some of my colleagues are women. It's not women's intelligence. It's women's psychology. Eh?"

He's being good-humored the only way he knows how. Don't hit him.

"What you've got to remember," said Ewing, energetically shredding a small napkin, "is that most women are liberated right now. They like what they're doing. They do it because they like it."

Don't, Janet.

"Not only that, you gals are going about it the wrong way."

You're in someone else's house. Be polite.

"You can't challenge men in their own fields," he said. "Now nobody can be more in favor of women getting their rights than I am. Do you want to sit down? Let's. As I said, I'm all in favor of it. Adds a decorative touch to the office, eh? Ha ha! Ha ha ha! Unequal pay is a disgrace. But you've got to remember, Janet, that women have certain physical limitations,"

43

(here he took off his glasses, wiped them with a little serrated square of blue cotton, and put them back on) "and you have to work within your physical limitations.

"For example," he went on, mistaking her silence for wisdom while Ludicrissa muttered, "How true! How true!" somewhere in the background about something or other, "you have to take into account that there are more than two thousand rapes in New York City alone in every particular year. I'm not saying of course that that's a good thing, but you have to take it into account. Men are physically stronger than women, you know."

(Picture me on the back of the couch, clinging to her hair like a homuncula, battering her on the top of the head until she doesn't dare to open her mouth.)

"Of course, Janet," he went on, "you're not one of those—uh—extremists. Those extremists don't take these things into account, do they? Of course not! Mind you, I'm not defending unequal pay but we have to take these things into account. Don't we? By the way, I make twenty thousand a year. Ha! Ha ha ha!" And off he went into another fit.

She squeaked something—because I was strangling her.

"What?" he said. "What did you say?" He looked at her nearsightedly. Our struggle must have imparted an unusual intensity to her expression because he seemed extraordinarily flattered by what he saw; he turned his head away coyly, sneaked a look out of the corner of his eye, and then whipped his head round into position very fast. As if he had been a bird.

"You're a good conversationalist," he said. He began to perspire gently. He shifted the pieces of his napkin from hand to hand. He dropped them and dusted his hands off. Now he's going to do it.

"Janet—uh—Janet, I wonder if you—" fumbling blindly for his drink—"that is if—uh—you—"

But we are far away, throwing coats out of the coat closet like a geyser.

Is that your method of courtship!

"Not exactly," I said. "You see—"

Baby, baby, baby. It's the host, drunk enough not to care.

Uh-oh. Be ladylike.

She showed him all her teeth. He saw a smile.

"You're beautiful, honey."

"Thank you. I go now." (good for her)

"Nah!" and he took us by the wrist. "Nah, you're not *going.*"

"Let me go," said Janet.

Say it loud. Somebody will come to rescue you.

Can't I rescue myself?

No.

Why not?

All this time he was nuzzling her ear and I was showing my distaste by shrinking terrified into a corner, one eye on the party. Everyone seemed amused.

"Give us a good-bye kiss," said the host, who might have been attractive under other circumstances, a giant marine, so to speak. I pushed him away.

"What'sa matter, you some kinda prude?" he said and enfolding us in his powerful arms, et cetera—well, not so very powerful as all that, but I want to give you the feeling of the scene. If you scream, people say you're melodramatic; if you submit, you're masochistic; if you call names, you're a bitch. Hit him and he'll kill you. The best thing is to suffer mutely and yearn for a rescuer, but suppose the rescuer doesn't come?

"Let go, ————," said Janet (some Russian word I didn't catch).

"Ha ha, make me," said the host, squeezing her wrist and puckering up his lips; "Make me, make me," and he swung his hips from side to side suggestively.

No, no, keep on being ladylike!

"Is this human courting?" shouted Janet. "Is this friendship? Is this politeness?" She had an extraordinarily loud voice. He laughed and shook her wrist.

"Savages!" she shouted. A hush had fallen on the party. The host leafed dexterously through his little book of rejoinders but did not come up with anything. Then he looked up "savage" only to find it marked with an affirmative: "Masculine, brute, virile, powerful, good." So he smiled broadly. He put the book away.

45

"Right on, sister," he said.

So she dumped him. It happened in a blur of speed and there he was on the carpet. He was flipping furiously through the pages of the book; what else is there to do in such circumstances? (It was a little limp-leather—excuse me—volume bound in blue, which I think they give out in high schools. On the cover was written in gold WHAT TO DO IN EVERY SITUATION.)

"Bitch!" (flip flip flip) "Prude!" (flip flip) "Ball-breaker!" (flip flip flip flip) "Goddamn cancerous castrator!" (flip) "Thinks hers is gold!" (flip flip) *"You didn't have to do that!"*

Was ist? said Janet in German.

He gave her to understand that she was going to die of cancer of the womb.

She laughed.

He gave her to understand further that she was taking unfair advantage of his good manners.

She roared.

He pursued the subject and told her that if he were not a gentleman he would ram her stinking, shitty teeth up her stinking shitty ass.

She shrugged.

He told her she was so ball-breaking, shitty, stone, scum-bag, mother-fucking, plug-ugly that no normal male could keep up an erection within half a mile of her.

She looked puzzled. ("Joanna, these are insults, yes?")

He got up. I think he was recovering his cool. He did not seem nearly so drunk as he had been. He shrugged his sports jacket back into position and brushed himself off. He said she had acted like a virgin, not knowing what to do when a guy made a pass, just like a Goddamned scared little baby virgin.

Most of us would have been content to leave it at that, eh, ladies?

Janet slapped him.

It was not meant to hurt, I think; it was a great big stinging theatrical performance, a cue for insults and further fighting, a come-on-get-your-guard con-

46

temptuous slap meant to enrage, which it jolly well did.

THE MARINE SAID, "YOU STUPID BROAD, I'M GONNA CREAM YOU!"

That poor man.

I didn't see things very well, as first off I got behind the closet door, but I saw him rush her and I saw her flip him; he got up again and again she deflected him, this time into the wall—I think she was worried because she didn't have time to glance behind her and the place was full of people—then he got up again and this time he swung instead and then something very complicated happened—he let out a yell and she was behind him, doing something cool and technical, frowning in concentration.

"Don't pull like that," she said. "You'll break your arm."

So he pulled. The little limp-leather notebook fluttered out on to the floor, from whence I picked it up. Everything was awfully quiet. The pain had stunned him, I guess.

She said in astonished good-humor: "But why do you want to fight when you do not know how?"

I got my coat and I got Janet's coat and I got us out of there and into the elevator. I put my head in my hands.

"Why'd you do it?"

"He called me a baby."

The little blue book was rattling around in my purse. I took it out and turned to the last thing he had said ("You stupid broad" et cetera). Underneath was written *Girl backs down—cries—manhood vindicated.* Under "Real Fight With Girl" was written *Don't hurt (except whores).* I took out my own pink book, for we all carry them, and turning to the instructions under "Brutality" found:

Man's bad temper is the woman's fault. It is also the woman's responsibility to patch things up afterwards.

There were sub-rubrics, one (reinforcing) under "Management" and one (exceptional) under "Martyrdom." Everything in my book begins with an M.

47

They do fit together so well, you know. I said to Janet:

"I don't think you're going to be happy here."

"Throw them both away, love," she answered.

III

Why make pretensions to fight (she said) when you can't fight? Why make pretensions to anything? I am trained, of course; that's my job, and it makes me the very devil angry when someone calls me names, but why call names? All this uneasy aggression. True, there is a little bit of hair-pulling on Whileaway, yes, and more than that, there is the temperamental thing, sometimes you can't stand another person. But the cure for that is distance. I've been foolish in the past, I admit. In middle-age one begins to settle down; Vittoria says I'm comic with my tohu-bohu when Yuki comes home with a hair out of place. I hope not. There is this thing with the child you've borne yourself, your body-child. There is also the feeling to be extra-proper in front of the children, yet hardly anybody bothers. Who has the time? And since I've become S & P I have a different outlook on all this: a job's a job and has to be done, but I don't like doing it for nothing, to raise the hand to someone. For sport, yes, okay, for hatred no. Separate them.

I ought to add there was a fourth duel in which nobody got killed; my opponent developed a lung infection, then a spinal infection—you understand, we weren't near civilization then—and the convalescence was such a long, nasty business. I took care of her. Nerve tissue's hard to regrow. She was paralyzed for a while, you know. Gave me a very salutary scare. So I don't fight with weapons now, except on my job, of course.

Am I sorry I hurt him?

Not me!

IV

Whileawayans are not nearly as peaceful as they sound.

V

Burned any bras lately har har twinkle twinkle A pretty girl like you doesn't need to be liberated twinkle har Don't listen to those hysterical bitches twinkle twinkle twinkle I never take a woman's advice about two things: love and automobiles twinkle twinkle har May I kiss your little hand twinkle twinkle twinkle. Har. Twinkle.

IV

On Whileaway they have a saying: When the mother and child are separated they both howl, the child because it is separated from the mother, the mother because she has to go back to work. Whileawayans bear their children at about thirty—singletons or twins as the demographic pressures require. These children have as one genotypic parent the biological mother (the "body-mother") while the non-bearing parent contributes the other ovum ("other mother"). Little Whileawayans are to their mothers both sulk and swank, fun and profit, pleasure and contemplation, a show of expensiveness, a slowing-down of life, an opportunity to pursue whatever interests the women have been forced to neglect previously, and the only leisure they have ever had—or will have again until old age. A family of thirty persons may have as many as four mother-and-child pairs in the common nursery at one time. Food, cleanliness, and shelter are not the mother's business; Whileawayans say with a straight face that she must be free to attend to the child's "finer spiritual needs." Then they go off by themselves and roar. The truth is they don't want to give up the leisure. Eventually we come to a painful scene. At the age of four or five these independent, blooming, pampered, extremely intelligent little girls are torn weeping and arguing from their thirty relatives and sent to the regional school, where they scheme and fight for weeks before giving in; some of them have been known to construct deadfalls or small bombs (having picked this knowledge up from their parents) in order to obliterate their instructors. Children are cared for in groups of five and taught in groups of differing sizes according to the subject under discussion. Their education at this point is heavily practical: how to run machines, how to get along without machines, law, transportation, physical theory, and so on. They learn gymnastics and mechanics. They learn practical medicine.

They learn how to swim and shoot. They continue (by themselves) to dance, to sing, to paint, to play, to do everything their Mommies did. At puberty they are invested with Middle-Dignity and turned loose; children have the right of food and lodging wherever they go, up to the power of the community to support them. They do not go back home.

Some do, of course, but then neither Mother may be there; people are busy; people are traveling; there's always work, and the big people who were so kind to a four-year-old have little time for an almost-adult. "And everything's so *small*," said one girl.

Some, wild with the desire for exploration, travel all around the world—usually in the company of other children—bands of children going to visit this or that, or bands of children about to reform the power installations, are a common sight on Whileaway.

The more profound abandon all possessions and live off the land just above or below the forty-eighth parallel; they return with animal heads, scars, visions.

50

Some make a beeline for their callings and spend most of puberty pestering part-time actors, bothering part-time musicians, cajoling part-time scholars.

Fools! (say the older children, who have been through it all) Don't be in such a hurry. You'll work soon enough.

At seventeen they achieve Three-Quarters Dignity and are assimilated into the labor force. This is probably the worst time in a Whileawayan's life. Groups of friends are kept together if the members request it and if it is possible, but otherwise these adolescents go where they're needed, not where they wish; nor can they join the Geographical Parliament nor the Professional Parliament until they have entered a family and developed that network of informal associations of the like-minded which is Whileaway's substitute for everything else but family.

They provide human companionship to Whileawayan cows, who pine and die unless spoken to affectionately.

They run routine machinery, dig people out of landslides, oversee food factories (with induction helmets on their heads, their toes controlling the greenpeas, their fingers the vats and controls, their back muscles the carrots, and their abdomens the water supply).

They lay pipe (again, by induction).

They fix machinery.

They are not allowed to have anything to do with malfunctions or breakdowns "on foot," as the Whileawayans say, meaning in one's own person and with tools in one's own hands, without the induction helmets that make it possible to operate dozens of waldoes at just about any distance you please. That's for veterans.

They do not meddle with computers "on foot" nor join with them via induction. That's for *old* veterans.

They learn to like a place only to be ordered somewhere else the next day, commandeered to excavate coastline or fertilize fields, kindly treated by the locals (if any) and hideously bored.

It gives them something to look forward to.

At twenty-two they achieve Full Dignity and may

either begin to learn the heretofore forbidden jobs or have their learning formally certificated. They are allowed to begin apprenticeships. They may marry into pre-existing families or form their own. Some braid their hair. By now the typical Whileawayan girl is able to do any job on the planet, except for specialties and extremely dangerous work. By twenty-five she has entered a family, thus choosing her geographical home base (Whileawayans travel all the time). Her family probably consists of twenty to thirty other persons, ranging in age from her own to the early fifties. (Families tend to age the way people do; thus new groupings are formed again in old age. Approximately every fourth girl must begin a new or join a nearly-new family.)

Sexual relations—which have begun at puberty—continue both inside the family and outside it, but mostly outside it. Whileawayans have two explanations for this. "Jealousy," they say for the first explanation, and for the second, "Why not?"

Whileawayan psychology locates the basis of Whileawayan character in the early indulgence, pleasure, and flowering which is drastically curtailed by the separation from the mothers. This (it says) gives Whileawayan life its characteristic independence, its dissatisfaction, its suspicion, and its tendency toward a rather irritable solipsism.

"Without which" (said the same Dunyasha Bernadetteson, q.v.) "we would all become contented slobs, *nicht wahr?*"

Eternal optimism hides behind this dissatisfaction, however; Whileawayans cannot forget that early paradise and every new face, every new day, every smoke, every dance, brings back life's possibilities. Also sleep and eating, sunrise, weather, the seasons, machinery, gossip, and the eternal temptations of art.

They work too much. They are incredibly tidy.

Yet on the old stone bridge that links New City, South Continent, with Varya's Little Alley Ho-ho is chiseled:

You never know what is enough until you know what is more than enough.

If one is lucky, one's hair turns white early; if—as

52

in old Chinese poetry—one is indulging oneself, one dreams of old age. For in old age the Whileawayan woman—no longer as strong and elastic as the young—has learned to join with calculating machines in the state they say can't be described but is most like a sneeze that never comes off. It is the old who are given the sedentary jobs, the old who can spend their days mapping, drawing, thinking, writing, collating, composing. In the libraries old hands come out from under the induction helmets and give you the reproductions of the books you want; old feet twinkle below the computer shelves, hanging down like Humpty Dumpty's; old ladies chuckle eerily while composing The Blasphemous Cantata (a great favorite of Ysaye's) or mad-moon cityscapes which turn out to be do-able after all; old brains use one part in fifty to run a city (with checkups made by two sulky youngsters) while the other forty-nine parts riot in a freedom they haven't had since adolescence.

The young are rather priggish about the old on Whileaway. They don't really approve of them.

Taboos on Whileaway: sexual relations with anybody considerably older or younger than oneself, waste, ignorance, offending others without intending to.

And of course the usual legal checks on murder and theft—both those crimes being actually quite difficult to commit. ("See," says Chilia, "it's murder if it's sneaky or if she doesn't want to fight. So you yell 'Olaf!' and when she turns around, then—")

No Whileawayan works more than three hours at a time on any one job, except in emergencies.

No Whileawayan marries monogamously. (Some restrict their sexual relations to one other person—at least while that other person is nearby—but there is no legal arrangement.) Whileawayan psychology again refers to the distrust of the mother and the reluctance to form a tie that will engage every level of emotion, all the person, all the time. And the necessity for artificial dissatisfactions.

"Without which" (says Dunyasha Bernadetteson, op. cit.) "we would become so happy we would sit

53

down on our fat, pretty behinds and soon we would start starving, *nyet?"*

But there is too, under it all, the incredible explosive energy, the gaiety of high intelligence, the obliquities of wit, the cast of mind that makes industrial areas into gardens and ha-has, that supports wells of wilderness where nobody ever lives for long, that strews across a planet sceneries, mountains, glider preserves, culs-de-sac, comic nude statuary, artistic lists of tautologies and circular mathematical proofs (over which aficionados are moved to tears), and the best graffiti in this or any other world.

Whileawayans work all the time. They work. And they work. *And they work.*

VII

Two ancients on the direct computer line between city and quarry (private persons have to be content with spark-gap radio), fighting at the top of their lungs while five green girls wait nearby, sulky and bored:

I can't make do with five greenies; I need two on-foot checkers and protective gear for one!

Can't have.

Incomp-

?

You hear.

Is me!

(affected disdain)

If catastroph—

Won't!

And so on.

VIII

A troop of little girls contemplating three silver hoops welded to a silver cube are laughing so hard that

54

some have fallen down into the autumn leaves on the plaza and are holding their stomachs. This is not embarrassment or an ignorant reaction to something new; they are genuine connoisseurs who have hiked for three days to see this. Their hip-packs lie around the edge of the plaza, near the fountains.

One: How lovely!

IX

Between shifts in the quarry in Newland, Henla Anaisson sings, her only audience her one fellow-worker.

X

A Belin, run mad and unable to bear the tediousness of her work, flees above the forty-eighth parallel, intending to remain there permanently. "You" (says an arrogant note she leaves behind) "do not exist" and although agreeing philosophically with this common view, the S & P for the county follows her—not to return her for rehabilitation, imprisonment, or study. What is there to rehabilitate or study? We'd all do it if we could. And imprisonment is simple cruelty.

You guessed it.

XI

"If not me or mine," (wrote Dunyasha Bernadetteson in 368 A.C.) "O.K.

"If me or mine—alas.

"If us and ours—*watch out!*"

XII

Whileaway is engaged in the reorganization of industry consequent to the discovery of the induction principle.

The Whileawayan work-week is sixteen hours.

PART FOUR

I

After six months of living with me in the hotel suite, Janet Evason expressed the desire to move in with a typical family. I heard her singing in the bathroom:

I know
That my
Rede-emer
Liveth
And She
Shall stand
Upon the latter da-ay   (ruffle)
On Earth.

"Janet?" She sang again (not badly) the second variation on the lines, in which the soprano begins to decorate the tune:

I know   (up)
Tha-at my   (ruffle)
Re-e-edeemer   (fiddle)
Liveth
And She
Shall stand   (convex)
And She
Shall stand   (concave)

"Janet, he's a Man!" I yelled. She went into the third variation, where the melody liquefies itself into its own adornments, very nice and quite improper:

I know   (up)
That my redee   (a high point, this one)
mer
Li-i-veth   (up up up)
And She
Shall stand   (hopefully)
And She shall stand   (higher)
Upon the la-a-a-a-atter da-a-a-y
                         (ruffle fiddle drip)
O-on Earth   (settling)

"JANET!" But of course she doesn't listen.

II

Whileawayans like big asses, so I am glad to report there was nothing of that kind in the family she moved in with. Father, mother, teenage daughter, and family dog were all delighted to be famous. Daughter was an honor student in the local high school. When Janet got settled I drifted into the attic; my spirit seized possession of the old four-poster bed stored next to the chimney, near the fur coats and the shopping bag full of dolls; and slowly, slowly, I infected the whole house.

III

Laura Rose Wilding of Anytown, U.S.A.
She has a black poodle who whines under the trees in the back yard and bares his teeth as he rolls over and over in the dead leaves. She's reading the Christian Existentialists for a course in school. She crosses the October weather, glowing with health, to

58

shake hands clumsily with Miss Evason. She's pathologically shy. She puts one hand in the pocket of her jeans, luminously, the way well-beloved or much-studied people do, tugging at the zipper of her man's leather jacket with the other hand. She has short sandy hair and freckles. Says over and over to herself Non Sum, Non Sum, which means either *I don't exist* or *I'm not that,* according to how you feel it; this is what Martin Luther is supposed to have said during his fit in the monastery choir.

"Can I go now?"

IV

The black poodle, Samuel, whined and scurried across the porch, then barked hysterically, defending the house against God-knows-what.

"At least she's White," they all said.

V

Janet, in her black-and-white tweeds with the fox collar like a movie star's, gave a speech to the local women's club. She didn't say much. Someone gave her chrysanthemums which she held upside-down like a baseball bat. A professor from the local college spoke of other cultures. A whole room was full of offerings brought by the club—brownies, fudge cake, sour cream cake, honey buns, pumpkin pie—not to be eaten, of course, only looked at, but they did eat it finally because somebody has to or it isn't real. "Hully gee, Mildred, you waxed the floor!" and she faints with happiness. Laur, who is reading psychology for the Existentialists (I said that, didn't I?), serves coffee to the club in the too-big man's shirt they can't ever get her out of, no matter what they do, and her ancient, shapeless jeans. Swaddling graveclothes. She's a bright girl. She learned in her thirteenth year that you can get old films of Mae West or Marlene Dietrich (who is a Vulcan; look at the eyebrows) after midnight on UHF if you know where to look, at fourteen that pot helps, at fifteen that reading's even better. She learned, wearing her rimless glasses, that the world is full of intelligent, attractive, talented women who manage to combine careers with their primary responsibilities as wives and mothers and whose husbands beat them. She's put a gold circle pin on her shirt as a concession to club day. She loves her father and once is enough. *Everyone knows* that much as women want to be scientists and engineers, they want foremost to be womanly companions to men (what?) and caretakers of childhood; *everyone knows* that a large part of a woman's identity inheres in the style of her attractiveness. Laur is daydreaming. She looks straight before her, blushes, smiles, and doesn't see a thing. After the party she'll march stiff-legged out of the room and up to her bedroom; sitting tailor-fashion on her bed, she'll read Engels on the family and make in the margin her neat, concise, perfectly written notes. She has shelves and shelves of such annotated works. Not for her "How true!!!!" or "oiseaux = birds." She's surrounded by mermaids, fish, sea-plants, wandering fronds. Drifting on the affective currents of the room are those strange social artifacts half dissolved in nature and mystery: *some pretty girls.*

Laur is daydreaming that she's Genghis Khan.

VI

A beautiful chick who swims naked and whose breasts float on the water like flowers, a chick in a rain-tight shirt who says she balls with her friends but doesn't get uptight about it, that's the real thing.

VII

And I like Anytown; I like going out on the porch at night to look at the lights of the town: fireflies in the blue gloaming, across the valley, up the hill, white homes where children played and rested, where wives made potato salad, home from a day in the autumn leaves chasing sticks with the family dog, families in the firelight, thousands upon thousands of identical, cozy days.

"Do you like it here?" asked Janet over dessert, never thinking that she might be lied to.

"Huh?" said Laur.

"Our guest wants to know if you like living here," said Mrs. Wilding.

"Yes," said Laur.

VIII

There are more whooping cranes in the United States of America than there are women in Congress.

IX

This then is Laura's worst mind: perpetually snowed in, a dim upstairs hall wrapped in cotton wool with Self counting rocks and shells in the window-seat. One can see nothing outside the glass but falling white sky—no footprints, no faces—though occasionally Self strays to the window, itself drowned in snowlight, and sees (or thinks she sees) in the petrified whirling waste the buried forms of two dead lovers, innocent and sexless, memorialized in a snowbank.

Turn away, girl; gird up your loins; go on reading.

X

Janet dreamed that she was skating backwards, Laura that a beautiful stranger was teaching her how to shoot. In dreams begin responsibilities. Laura came down to the breakfast table after everybody had gone except Miss Evason. Whileawayans practice secret dream interpretation according to an arbitrary scheme they consider idiotic but very funny; Janet was guiltily seeing how contrary she could make her dream come out and giggling around her buttered toast. She snickered and shed crumbs. When Laura came into the room Janet sat up straight and didn't guffaw. "I," said Laur severely, the victim of ventriloquism, "detest women who don't know how to be women." Janet and I said nothing. We noticed the floss and dew on the back of her neck—Laur is in some ways more like a thirteen-year-old than a seventeen-year-old. She mugs, for instance. At sixty Janet will be white-haired and skinny, with surprised blue eyes—quite a handsome human being. And Janet herself always likes people best as themselves, not dressed up, so Laur's big shirt tickled her, ditto those impossible trousers. She wanted to ask if it was one shirt or many; do you scream when you catch sight of yourself?

She soberly held out a piece of buttered toast and Laur took it with a grimace.

"I don't," said Laur in an entirely different tone, "understand where the devil they all go on Saturday mornings. You'd think they were trying to catch up with the sun." Sharp and adult.

"I dreamed I was learning to use a rifle," she added. We thought of confiding to her the secret dream-system by which Whileawayans transform matter and embrace the galaxies but then we thought better of it.

62

Janet was trying in a baffled way to pick up the crumbs she had dropped; Whileawayans don't eat crunchables. I left her and floated up to the whatnot, on which were perched two biscuit-china birds, beak twined in beak, a cut-glass salt dish, a small, wooden Mexican hat, a miniature silver basket, and a terracotta ashtray shaped realistically like a camel. Laur looked up for a moment, preternaturally hard and composed. I am a spirit, remember. She said: "The hell with it."

"What?" said Janet. This response is considered quite polite on Whileaway. I, the plague system darting in the air between them, pinched Janet's ears, plucked them up like Death in the poem. Nowhere, neither undersea nor on the moon, have I, in my bodiless wanderings, met with a more hard-headed innocence than Miss Evason brings to the handling of her affairs. In the bluntness of her imagination she unbuttoned Laur's shirt and slid her pants down to her knees. The taboos in Whileawayan society are cross-age taboos. Miss Evason no longer smiled.

"I said the hell with it," the little girl repeated aggressively.

"You said—?"

(Imitation Laura was smiling helplessly and freshly over her shoulder, shivering a little as her breasts were touched. What we like is the look of affection.)

She studied her plate. She drew a design on it with her finger. "Nothing," she said. "I want to show you something."

"Show, then," said Janet. I bet your knees turn in. Janet didn't think so. There are these fashion magazines scattered through the house, Mrs. Wilding reads them, pornography for the high-minded. Girls in wet knit bathing suits with their hair dripping, silly girls drowned in sweaters, serious girls in backless jersey evening dresses that barely cover the fine-boned lyres of their small chests. They're all slim and young. Pushing and prodding the little girl as you fit a dress on her. Stand here. Stand there. How, swooning, they fell into each other's arms. Janet, who (unlike me) never imagines what can't be done, wiped her mouth, folded her napkin, pushed back her chair, got up, and followed

63

Laur into the living room. Up the stairs. Laur took a notebook from her desk and handed it to Miss Evason. We stood there uncertainly, ready to laugh or cry; Janet looked down at the manuscript, up over the edge at Laura, down again for a few more lines. Peek.

"I can't read this," I said.

Laura raised her eyebrows severely.

"I know the language but not the context," Janet said. "I can't judge this, child."

Laura frowned. I thought she might wring her hands but no such luck. She went back to the desk and picked up something else, which she handed to Miss Evason. I knew enough to recognize mathematics, that's all. She tried to stare Janet down. Janet followed a few lines, smiled thoughtfully, then came to a hitch. Something wrong. "Your teacher—" began Miss Evason.

"I don't have a teacher," said perspicacious Laur. "I do it myself, out of the book."

"Then the book's wrong," said Janet; "Look," and she proceeded to scribble in the margin. What an extraordinary phenomenon mathematical symbols are! I flew to the curtains, curtains Mrs. Wilding had washed and ironed with her own hands. No, she took them to the cleaner's, popping the clutch of the Wildings' station wagon. She read Freud in the time she would have used to wash and iron the curtains. They weren't Laur's choice. She would have torn them down with her own hands. She wept. She pleaded. She fainted. Et cetera.

They bent over the book together.

"Goddamn," said Janet, in surprised pleasure.

"You know math!" (that was Laur).

"No, no, I'm just an amateur, just an amateur," said Miss Evason, swimming like a seal in the sea of numbers.

"The life so short, the craft so long to learn," quoted Laur and turned scarlet. The rest goes: *I mene love.*

"What?" said Janet, absorbed.

"I'm in love with someone in school," said Laur. "A man."

A really extraordinary expression, what they mean by calling someone's face *a study*—she can't know

64

that I know that she doesn't know that I know!—crossed Janet's face and she said, "Oh, sure," by which you can tell that she didn't believe a word of it. She didn't say, "You're too young." (Not for him, for her, nitwit).

"Of course," she added.

XI

I'm a victim of penis envy (said Laura) so I can't ever be happy or lead a normal life. My mother worked as a librarian when I was little and that's not feminine. She thinks it's deformed me. The other day a man came up to me in the bus and called me sweetie and said, "Why don't you smile? God loves you!" I just stared at him. But he wouldn't go away until I smiled, so finally I did. Everyone was laughing. I tried once, you know, went to a dance all dressed up, but I felt like such a fool. Everyone kept making encouraging remarks about my looks as if they were afraid I'd cross back over the line again; I was *trying*, you know, I was proving their way of life was right, and they were terrified I'd stop. When I was five I said, "I'm not a girl, I'm a genius," but that doesn't work, possibly because other people don't honor the resolve. Last year I finally gave up and told my mother I didn't want to be a girl but she said Oh no, being a girl is wonderful. Why? Because you can wear pretty clothes and you don't have to do anything; the men will do it for you. She said that instead of conquering Everest, I could conquer the conqueror of Everest and while he had to go climb the mountain, I could stay home in lazy comfort listening to the radio and eating chocolates. She was upset, I suppose, but you can't imbibe someone's success by fucking them. Then she said that in addition to that (the pretty clothes and so forth) there is a mystical fulfillment in marriage and children that nobody who hasn't done it could ever know. "Sure, washing floors," I said. "I have

65

you," she said, looking mysterious. As if my father
didn't have me, too. Or my birth was a beautiful
experience *et patati et patata,* which doesn't quite jibe
with the secular version we always get when she's talking about her ailments with her friends. When I was a
little girl I used to think women were always sick. My
father said, "What the hell is she fussing about this
time?" All those songs, what's-its-name, I enjoy being a
girl, I'm so glad I'm female, I'm all dressed up, Love
will make up for everything, tra-la-la. Where are the
songs about how glad I am I'm a boy? Finding The
Man. Keeping The Man. Not scaring The Man, building up The Man, pleasing The Man, interesting The
Man, following The Man, soothing The Man, flattering
The Man, deferring to The Man, changing your judgment for The Man, changing your decisions for The
Man, polishing floors for The Man, being perpetually
conscious of your appearance for The Man, being romantic for The Man, hinting to The Man, losing yourself in The Man. "I never had a thought that wasn't
yours." Sob, sob. Whenever I act like a human being,
they say, "What are you getting upset about?" They
say: of course you'll get married. They say: of course
you're brilliant. They say: of course you'll get a Ph.D.
and then sacrifice it to have babies. They say: if you
don't, you're the one who'll have two jobs and you can
make a go of it if you're exceptional, which very few
women are, *and if you find a very understanding man.*
As long as you don't make more money than he does.
How do they expect me to live all this junk? I went to
a Socialist—not really Socialist, you understand—camp
for two summers; my parents say I must have gotten
my crazy ideas there. Like hell I did. When I was thirteen my uncle wanted to kiss me and when I tried to
run away, everybody laughed. He pinned my arms and
kissed me on the cheek; then he said, "Oho, I got my
kiss! I got my kiss!" and everybody thought it was too
ducky for words. Of course they blamed me—it's
harmless, they said, you're only a child, he's paying
you attention; you ought to be grateful. Everything's all
right as long as he doesn't rape you. Women only have
feelings; men have *egos.* The school psychologist told

66

me I might not realize it, but I was living a very dangerous style of life that might in time lead to Lesbianism (ha! ha!) and I should try to look and act more feminine. I laughed until I cried. Then he said I must understand that femininity was a Good Thing, and although men's and women's functions in society were different, they had equal dignity. Separate but equal, right? Men make the decisions and women make the dinners. I expected him to start in about that mystically-wonderful-experience-which-no-man-can-know crap, but he didn't. Instead he took me to the window and showed me the expensive clothing stores across the way. Then he said, "See, it's a woman's world, after all." The pretty clothes again. I thought some damn horrible thing was going to happen to me right there on his carpet. I couldn't talk. I couldn't move. I felt deathly sick. He really expected me to live like that— he looked at me and that's what he saw, after eleven months. He expected me to start singing "I'm So Glad I'm A Girl" right there in his Goddamned office. And a little buck-and-wing. And a little nigger shuffle.

"Would *you* like to live like that?" I said.

He said, "That's irrelevant, because I'm a man."

I haven't the right hobbies, you see. My hobby is mathematics, not boys. And being young, too, that's a drag. You have to take all kinds of crap.

Boys don't like smart girls. Boys don't like aggressive girls. Unless they want to sit in the girls' laps, that is. I never met a man yet who wanted to make it with a female Genghis Khan. Either they try to dominate you, which is revolting, or they turn into babies. You might as well give up. Then I had a lady shrink who said it was my problem because I was the one who was trying to rock the boat and *you can't expect them to change.* So I suppose I'm the one who must change. Which is what my best friend said. "Compromise," she said, answering her fiftieth phone call of the night. "Think what power it gives you over them."

Them! Always Them, Them, Them. I can't just think of myself. My mother thinks that I *don't like boys,* though I try to tell her: Look at it this way; I'll never lose my virginity. I'm a Man-Hating Woman and people leave the room when I come in it. Do they do the same for a Woman-Hating Man? Don't be silly.

She'll never know—nor would she credit if she knew—that men sometimes look very beautiful to me. From the depths, looking up.

There was a very nice boy once who said, "Don't worry, Laura. I know you're really very sweet and gentle underneath." And another with, "You're strong, like an earth mother." And a third, "You're so beautiful when you're angry." My guts on the floor, you're so beautiful when you're angry. *I want to be recognized.*

I've never slept with a girl. I couldn't. I wouldn't want to. That's abnormal and I'm not, although you can't be normal unless you do what you want and you can't be normal unless you love men. To do what I wanted would be normal, unless what I wanted was abnormal, in which case it would be abnormal to please myself and normal to do what I didn't want to do, which isn't normal.

So you see.

XII

Dunyasha Bernadetteson (the most brilliant mind in the world, b. A.C. 344, d. A.C. 426) heard of this unfortunate young person and immediately pronounced the following *shchasniy,* or cryptic one-word saying:
"Power!"

XIII

We persevered, reading magazines and covering the neighbors' activities in the discreetest way possible, and Janet—who didn't believe us to be fully human—kept her affections to herself. She got used to Laur's standing by the door every time we went out in the evening with a stubborn look on her face as if she were going to fling herself across the door with her arms spread out, movie style. But Laur controlled herself. Janet went out on a few arranged dates with local men but awe silenced them; she learned nothing of the usual way such things were done. She went to a high school basketball game (for the boys) and a Fashion Fair (for the girls). There was a Science Fair, whose misconceptions she enjoyed mightily. Like oil around water, the community parted to let us through.

Laura Rose came up to Miss Evason one night as the latter sat reading alone in the living room; it was February and the soft snow clung to the outside of the picture window. Picture windows in Anytown do not evaporate snow in the wintertime as windows do on Whileaway. Laur watched us standoffishly for a while, then came into the circle of fantasy and lamplight. She stood there, twisting her class ring around her finger. Then she said:

"What have you learned from all that reading?"

"Nothing," said Janet. The soundless blows of the snowflakes against the glass. Laur sat down at Janet's feet ("Shall I tell you something?") and explained an old fantasy of hers, snow and forests and knights and lovelorn maidens. She said that to anyone in love the house would instantly seem submarine, not a house on Earth but a house on Titan under the ammonia snow. "I'm in love," she said, reviving that old story about the mythical man at school.

"Tell me about Whileaway," she added. Janet put down her magazine. Indirection is so new to Miss Evason that for a moment she doesn't understand; what Laur has said is: *Tell me about your wife.* Janet was pleased. She had traced Laur's scheme not as concealment but as a kind of elaborate frivolity; now she fell silent. The little girl sat tailor-fashion on the living room rug, watching us.

"Well, tell me," said Laura Rose.

Her features are delicate, not particularly marked; she has a slightly indecently milky skin and lots of freckles. Knobby knuckles.

"She's called Vittoria," said Janet—how crude,

69

once said!—and there goes something in Laura Rose's heart, like the blows of something light but perpetually shocking: oh! oh! oh! She reddened and said something very faintly, something I lip-read but didn't hear. Then she put her hand on Janet's knee, a hot, moist hand with its square fingers and stubby nails, a hand of tremendous youthful presence, and said something else, still inaudible.

Leave! (I told my compatriot)

First of all, it's wrong.

Second of all, it's wrong.

Third of all, it's wrong.

"Oh my goodness," said Janet slowly, as she does sometimes, this being her favorite saying after, "You are kidding me."

(Performing the difficult mental trick of trying on somebody else's taboos.)

"Now then," she said, "now then, now then." The little girl looked up. She is in the middle of something terribly distressing, something that will make her wring her hands, will make her cry. As a large Irish setter once bounded into my room and spent half the day unconsciously banging a piece of furniture with his tail; so something awful has got into Laura Rose and is giving her electric shocks, terrifying blows, right across the heart. Janet took her by the shoulders and it got worse. There is this business of the narcissism of love, the fourth-dimensional curve that takes you out into the other who is the whole world, which is really a twist back into yourself, only a different self. Laur was weeping with despair. Janet pulled her up on to her lap—Janet's lap—as if she had been a baby; *everyone knows* that if you start them young they'll be perverted forever and *everyone knows* that nothing in the world is worse than making love to someone a generation younger than yourself. Poor Laura, defeated by both of us, her back bent, glazed and stupefied under the weight of a double taboo.

Don't, Janet.

Don't, Janet.

Don't exploit. That little girl's sinister wisdom.

Snow still blew across the side of the house; the

walls shook, muffled. Something was wrong with the television set, or with the distance control, or perhaps some defective appliance somewhere in suburban Anytown sent out uncontrolled signals that no television set could resist; for it turned itself on and gave us a television salad: Maureen trying unsuccessfully to slap John Wayne, a pretty girl with a drowned voice holding up a vaginal deodorant spray can, a house falling off the side of a mountain. Laur groaned aloud and hid her face against Janet's shoulder. Janet—I—held her, her odor flooding my skin, cold woman, grinning at my own desire because we are still trying to be good. Whileawayans, as has been said, love big asses. "I love you, I love you," said Laur, and Janet rocked her, and Laur—not wishing to be taken for a child—bent Miss Evason's head fiercely back against the chair and kissed her on the mouth. Oh my goodness.

Janet's rid of me. I sprang away and hung by one claw from the window curtain. Janet picked Laur up and deposited her on the floor, holding her tight through all the hysterics; she nuzzled Laur's ear and slipped off her own shoes. Laur came up out of it and threw the distance control at the television set, for the actress had been telling you to disinfect the little-mouse "most girl part" and the set went dead.

"Never—don't—I can't—leave me!" wailed Laur. Better to cry. Businesslike Janet unfastened her shirt, her belt, and her blue jeans and gripped her about the hips, on the theory that nothing calms hysterics so fast.

"Oh!" said Laura Rose, astounded. This is the perfect time for her to change her mind. Her breathing grew quieter. Soberly she put her arms around Janet and leaned on Janet. She sighed.

"I want to get out of my damned clothes," said Janet, voice unaccountably breaking in the middle.

"Do you love me?"

Dearest, I can't because you are too young; and some day soon you'll look at me and my skin will be dead and dry, and being more romantically inclined than a Whileawayan, you'll find me quite disgusting; but until then I'll do my best to conceal from you how very fond I am of you. There is also lust and I hope

71

you understand me when I say I'm about to die; and I think we should go to a safer place where we can die in comfort, for example my room which has a lock on the door, because I don't want to be panting away on the rug when your parents walk in. On Whileaway it wouldn't matter and you wouldn't have parents at your age, but here—or so I'm told—things are as they are.

"What a strange and lovely way you have of putting it," Laur said. They climbed the stairs, Laur worrying a bit at her trailing pants. She bent down (framed in the doorway) to rub her ankles. She's going to laugh in a minute and look at us from between her legs. She straightened up with a shy smile.

"Tell me something," she said in a hoarse, difficult whisper, averting her gaze.

"Yes, child? Yes, dear?"

"What do we do now?"

XIV

They undressed in Janet's bedroom in the midst of her piles of material: books, magazines, sources of statistics, biographies, newspapers. The ghosts in the windowpanes undressed with them, for nobody could see in at the back of the house. Their dim and pretty selves. Janet pulled down the shades, lingering at each window and peering wistfully out into the dark, a shocking compound of familiar, friendly face and awful nude, while Laur climbed into Janet's bed. The bedspread had holes in it where the pink satin had worn thin. She shut her eyes. "Put out the light."

"Oh no, please," said Janet, making the bed sway by getting into it. She held out her arms to the little girl; then she kissed her on the shoulder, the Russian way. (She's the wrong shape.) "I don't want the light," said Laur and jumped out of bed to turn it off, but the air catches you on your bare skin before you get there and shocks you out of your senses; so she stopped, mother-naked, with the currents of air investigating between her legs. "How lovely!" said Janet. The room is pitilessly well lit. Laur got back into bed—"Move over"—and that awful sensation that you're not going to enjoy it after all. "You have lovely knees," Janet said mildly, "and such a beautiful rump," and for a moment the preposterousness of it braced Laura Rose; there couldn't be any sex in it; so she turned off the overhead light and got back into bed. Janet had turned on a rose-shaded night lamp by the bed. Miss Evason grew out of the satin cover, an antique statue from the waist up with preternaturally living eyes; she said softly, "Look, we're alike, aren't we?" indicating her round breasts, idealized by the dimness. "I've had two children," she said wickedly and Laur felt herself go red all over, so unpleasant was the picture of Yuriko Janetson being held up to one breast to suck, not, it seemed to Laur, an uncollected, starry-eyed infant but something like a miniature adult, on a ladder perhaps. Laur lay stiffly back and shut her eyes, radiating refusal.

Janet turned out the bedside light.

Miss Evason then pulled the covers up around her shoulders, sighed in self-control, and ordered Laur to turn over. "You can at least get a back-rub out of it."

"Ugh!" she said sincerely, when she began on the muscles of Laura's neck. "What a mess."

Laura tried to giggle. Miss Evason's voice, in the darkness, went on and on: about the last few weeks, about studying freshwater ponds on Whileaway, a hard, lean, sexless greyhound of a voice (Laur thought) which betrayed Laura in the end, Miss Evason stating with an odd, unserious chuckle, "Try?"

"I do love you," Laur said, ready to weep. There is propaganda and propaganda and I represented again to Janet that what she was about to do was a serious crime.

God will punish, I said.

You are supposed to make them giggle, but Janet remembered how she herself had been at twelve, and oh it's so serious. She kissed Laura Rose lightly on the lips over and over again until Laura caught her head; in the dark it wasn't really so bad and Laura could imagine that she was nobody, or that Miss Evason was nobody, or that she was imagining it all. One nice thing to do is rub from the neck down to the tail, it renders the human body ductile and makes the muscles purr. Without knowing it, Laur was in over her head. She had learned from a boy friend how to kiss on top, but here there was lots of time and lots of other places; "It's *nice!*" said Laura Rose in surprise; "It's so *nice!*" and the sound of her own voice sent her in head over heels. Janet found the little bump Whileawayans call The Key—*Now you must make an effort,* she said—and with the sense of working very hard, Laur finally tumbled off the cliff. It was incompletely and desperately inadequate, but it was the first major sexual pleasure she had ever received from another human being in her entire life.

"Goddammit, I *can't!*" she shouted.

So I fled shrieking. There is no excuse for putting my face between someone else's columnar thighs—picture me as washing my cheeks and temples outside to get rid of that cool smoothness (cool because of the fat, you see, that insulates the limbs; you can almost feel the long bones, the *architectura,* the heavenly technical cunning. They'll be doing it with the dog next). I sat on the hall window frame and screamed.

Janet must be imagined throughout as practicing the extremest self-control.

What else can she do?

"Now do this and this," she whispered hurriedly to Laura Rose, laughing brokenly. "Now do that and that. Ah!" Miss Evason used the girl's ignorant hand, for Laura didn't know how to do it; "Just hold still," she said in that strange parody of an intimate confession. The girl's inexperience didn't make things easy. However, one finds one's own rhythm. In the bottom drawer of the Wildings' guest room bureau was an exotic Whileawayan artifact (with a handle) that Laura Rose is going to be very embarrassed to see the next morning; Janet got it out, wobbling drunkenly.

("Did you fall down?" said Laura anxiously, leaning over the edge of the bed.

("Yes.")

So it was easy. Touched with strange inspiration,

74

Laur held the interloper in her arms, awed, impressed, a little domineering. Months of chastity went up in smoke: an electrical charge, the wriggling of an internal eel, a knifelike pleasure.

"No, no, not yet," said Janet Evason Belin. "Just hold it. Let me rest."

"Now. Again."

XV

A dozen beautiful "girls" each "brushing" and "combing" her long, silky "hair," each "longing" to "catch a man."

XVI

I fell in love at twenty-two.

A dreadful intrusion, a sickness. Vittoria, whom I did not even know. The trees, the bushes, the sky, were all sick with love. The worst thing (said Janet) is the intense familiarity, the sleepwalker's conviction of having blundered into an eruption of one's own inner life, the yellow-pollinating evergreen brushed and sticky with my own good humor, the flakes of myself falling invisibly from the sky to melt on my own face.

In your terms, I was distractedly in love. Whileawayans account for cases of this by referring back to the mother-child relationship: cold potatoes when you feel it. There used to be an explanation by way of our defects, but common human defects can be used to explain anything, so what's the use. And there's a mathematical analogy, a four-dimensional curve that I remember laughing at. Oh, I was bleeding to death.

Love—to work like a slave, to work like a dog. The same exalted, feverish attention fixed on everything. I didn't make a sign to her because she didn't make a sign to me; I only tried to control myself and to keep people away from me. That awful diffidence. I was *at her* too, all the time, in a nervous parody of friendship. Nobody can be expected to like that compulsiveness. In our family hall, like the Viking meadhall where the bird flies in from darkness and out again into darkness, under the blown-up pressure dome with the fans bringing in the scent of roses, I felt my own soul fly straight up into the roof. We used to sit with the lights off in the long spring twilight; a troop of children had passed by the week before, selling candles, which one or another woman would bring in and light. People drifted in and out, lifting the silk flap to the dome entrance. People ate at different times, you see. When Vitti left for outside, I followed her. We don't have lawns as you do, but around our dwellings we plant a kind of trefoil which keeps the other things off; small children always assume it's there for magical reasons. It's very soft. It was getting dark, too. There's a planting from New Forest near the farmhouse and we wandered toward it, Vitti idle and saying nothing.

"I'll be leaving in six months," I said. "Going to New City to get tied in with the power plants."

Silence. I was miserably conscious that Vittoria was going somewhere and I should know where because someone had told me, but I couldn't remember.

"I thought you might like company," I said.

No answer. She had picked up a stick and was taking the heads off weeds with it. It was one of the props for the computer receiver pole, knocked into the ground at one end and into the pole itself at the other. I had to ignore her being there or I couldn't have continued walking. Ahead were the farm's trees, breaking into the fields on the dim horizon like a headland or a cloud. "The moon's up," I said. See the moon. Poisoned with arrows and roses, radiant Eros coming at you out of the dark. The air so mild you could bathe in it. I'm told my first sentence as a child was See the Moon, by which I think I must have meant: pleasant pain, balmy poison, preserving gall, choking sweet. I imagined Vittoria cutting her way out of the night with that stick, whirling it around her head, leaving bruises

76

in the earth, tearing up weeds, slashing to pieces the roses that climbed around the computer poles. There was no part of my mind exempt from the thought: if she moves in this quicksilver death, it'll kill me.

We reached the trees. (I remember, she's going to Lode-Pigro to put up buildings. Also, it'll be hotter here in July. It'll be intensely hot, probably not bearable.) The ground between them was carpeted in needles, speckled with moonlight. We dissolved fantastically into that extraordinary medium, like mermaids, like living stories; I couldn't see anything. There was the musky odor of dead needles, although the pollen itself is scentless. If I had told her, "Vittoria, I'm very fond of you," or "Vittoria, I love you," she might answer, "You're O.K. too, friend," or "Yes, sure, let's make it," which would misrepresent something or other, though I don't know just what, quite intolerably and I would have to kill myself—I was very odd about death in those strange days. So I did not speak or make a sign but only strolled on, deeper and deeper into that fantastic forest, that enchanted allegory, and finally we came across a fallen log and sat on it.

"You'll miss—" said Vitti.

I said, "Vitti, I want—"

She stared straight ahead, as if displeased. Sex does not matter in these things, nor age, nor time, nor sense, we all know that. In the daytime you can see that the trees have been planted in straight rows, but the moonlight was confusing all that.

A long pause here.

"I don't know you," I said at last. The truth was we had been friends for a long time, good friends. I don't know why I had forgotten that so completely. Vitti was the anchor in my life at school, the chum, the pal; we had gossiped together, eaten together. I knew nothing about her thoughts now and can't report them, except for my own fatuous remarks. Oh, the dead silence! I groped for her hand but couldn't find it in the dark; I cursed myself and tried to stay together in that ghastly moonlight, shivers of unbeing running through me like a net and over all the pleasure of pain, the dreadful longing.

"Vitti, I love you."

Go away! Was she wringing her hands?

"Love me!"

No! and she threw one arm up to cover her face. I got down on my knees but she winced away with a kind of hissing screech, very like the sound an enraged gander makes to warn you and be fair. We were both shaking from head to foot. It seemed natural that she should be ready to destroy me. I've dreamed of looking into a mirror and seeing my alter ego which, on its own initiative, begins to tell me unbearable truths and, to prevent such, threw my arms around Vittoria's knees while she dug her fingers into my hair; thus connected we slid down to the forest floor. I expected her to beat my head against it. We got more equally together and kissed each other, I expecting my soul to flee out of my body, which it did not do. She is untouchable. What can I do with my dearest X, Y, or Z, after all? This is Vitti, whom I know, whom I like; and the warmth of that real affection inspired me with more love, the love with more passion, more despair, enough disappointment for a whole lifetime. I groaned miserably. I might as well have fallen in love with a tree or a rock. No one can make love in such a state. Vitti's fingernails were making little hard crescents of pain on my arms; she had that mulish look I knew so well in her; I knew something was coming off. It seemed to me that we were victims of the same catastrophe and that we ought to get together somewhere, in a hollow tree or under a bush, to talk it over. The old women tell you to wrestle, not fight, or you may end up with a black eye; Vitti, who had my fingers in her hands, pressing them feverishly, bent the smallest one back against the joint. Now that's a good idea. We scuffled like babies, hurting my hand, and she bit me on it; we pushed and pulled at each other, and I shook her until she rolled over on top of me and very earnestly hit me across the face with her fist. The only relief is tears. We lay sobbing together. What we did after that I think you know, and we sniffled and commiserated with each other. It even struck us funny, once. The seat of romantic love is the solar plexus while the seat of love is elsewhere, and that makes it very hard to *make love* when you are on the point of dissolution, your arms and legs penetrated by moonlight, your head cut off and swimming freely on its own like some kind of mutated monster. Love is a radiation disease. Whileawayans do not like the self-consequence that comes with romantic passion and we are very mean and mocking about it; so Vittoria and I walked back separately, each frightened to death of the weeks and weeks yet to go before we'd be over it. We kept it to ourselves. I felt it leave me two and a half months later, at one particular point in time: I was putting a handful of cracked corn to my mouth and licking the sludge off my fingers. I felt the parasite go. I swallowed philosophically and that was that. I didn't even have to tell her.

Vitti and I have stayed together in a more commonplace way ever since. In fact, we got married. It comes and goes, that abyss opening on nothing. I run away, usually.

Vittoria is whoring all over North Continent by now, I should think. We don't mean by that what you do, by the way. I mean: good for her.

Sometimes I try to puzzle out the different kinds of love, the friendly kind and the operatic kind, but what the hell.

Let's go to sleep.

XVII

Under the Mashopi mountain range is a town called Wounded Knee and beyond this the agricultural plain of Green Bay. Janet could not have told you where the equivalents of these landmarks are in the here-and-now of our world and neither can I, the author. In the great terra-reforming convulsion of P.C. 400 the names themselves dissolved into the general mess of re-crystallization so that it would be impossible for any Whileawayan to tell you (if you were to ask) whether Mashopi was ever a city, or Wounded Knee a

kind of bush, or whether or not Green Bay was ever a
real bay. But if you go South from the Altiplano over the
Mashopi Range, and from that land of snow, cold, thin
air, risk, and glaciers, to the glider resort at Utica (from
whence you may see mountain climbers setting off for
Old Dirty-Skirts, who stands twenty-three thousand,
nine hundred feet high) and from there to the monorail
station at Wounded Knee, and if you take the monorail
eight hundred miles into Green Bay and get off at a station I won't name, you'll be where Janet was when she
had just turned seventeen. A Whileawayan who had
come from the Mars training settlement in the Altiplano would have thought Green Bay was heaven; a
hiker out of New Forest would have hated it. Janet had
come by herself from an undersea farm on the conti-
nental shelf on the other side of the Altiplano where
she had spent five wretched weeks setting up machinery
in inaccessible crannies and squeaking whenever she
talked (because of the helium). She had left her schoolmates there, crazy for space and altitude. It's not usual
to be alone at that age. She had stayed at the hostel in
Wounded Knee, where they gave her an old, unused
cubicle from which she could work by induction in the
fuel-alcohol distillery. People were nice, but it was a
miserable and boring time. You are never so alone,
schoolmates or not. You never feel so all-thumbs
(Janet). She made her insistence on change formally,
the line of work came through, goodbye everybody.
She had left a violin in Wounded Knee with a friend
who used to cantilever herself out of the third story of
the hostel and eat snacks on the head of a public
statue. Janet took the monorail at twenty-two o'clock
and sulkily departed for a better personal world. There
were four persons of Three-Quarters Dignity in the car,
all quiet, all wretched with discontent. She opened her
knapsack, wrapped herself in it, and slept. She woke in
artificial light to find that the engineer had opened the
louvers to let in April: magnolias were blooming in
Green Bay. She played linear poker with an old woman
from the Altiplano who beat her three times out of three.
At dawn everyone was asleep and the lights winked
out; she woke and watched the low hills form and

re-form outside under an apple-green sky that turned, as she watched it, a slow, sulphurous yellow. It rained but they sped through it. At the station—which was nothing but the middle of a field—she borrowed a bicycle from the bicycle rack and flipped the toggle to indicate the place she wanted to go. It's a stout machine, with broad tires (compared to ours) and a receiver for registering radio beacons. She rode into the remaining night hung between the plantations of evergreens, then out into the sunrise again. There was an almighty cheeping and chirping, the result of one limb of the sun becoming visible over the horizon. She could see the inflated main dome of the house before she reached the second bicycle drop; somebody going West would pick it up in time and drop it near the monorail. She imagined great masses of sulky girls being requisitioned to ride bicycles coast-to-coast from regions that had a bicycle surplus to those crying out for bicycles. I imagined it, too. There was the sound of a machinist's ground-car off to the left—Janet grew up with that noise in her ears. Her bicycle was singing the musical tone that lets you know you're on course, a very lovely sound to hear over the empty fields. "Sh!" she said and put it on the rack, where it obediently became silent. She walked (and so did I) to the main dome of the house and let herself in, not knowing whether everyone was sleeping late or had got up early and already gone out. She didn't care. We found the empty guest room, ate some stirabout—that's not what you think, it's a kind of bread—from her knapsack, lay down on the floor, and fell asleep.

XVIII

There's no being *out too late* in Whileaway, or *up too early*, or *in the wrong part of town*, or *unescorted*. You cannot fall out of the kinship web and become sexual prey for strangers, for there is no prey and there are no strangers—the web is world-wide. In all of

Whileaway there is no one who can keep you from going where you please (though you may risk your life, if that sort of thing appeals to you), no one who will follow you and try to embarrass you by whispering obscenities in your ear, no one who will attempt to rape you, no one who will warn you of the dangers of the street, no one who will stand on street corners, hot-eyed and vicious, jingling loose change in his pants pocket, bitterly bitterly sure that you're a cheap floozy, hot and wild, who likes it, who can't say no, who's making a mint off it, who inspires him with nothing but disgust, and who wants to drive him crazy.

On Whileaway eleven-year-old children strip and live naked in the wilderness above the forty-seventh parallel, where they meditate, stark naked or covered with leaves, *sans* pubic hair, subsisting on the roots and berries so kindly planted by their elders. You can walk around the Whileawayan equator twenty times (if the feat takes your fancy and you live that long) with one hand on your sex and in the other an emerald the size of a grapefruit. All you'll get is a tired wrist.

While here, where *we* live—!

PART FIVE

I

I had got stuck with Jeannine. I don't know how. Also, everybody in the Goddamned subway car was staring at my legs. I think they thought I was a cheerleader. Way up in the Bronx we had waited for the Express, forty-five minutes in the open air with tufts of grass growing between the rails, just as in my childhood, weeds surrounding the vacant subway cars, sunlight and cloud-shadows chasing each other across the elevated wooden platform. I put my raincoat across my knees—skirts are long in nineteen-sixty-nine, Jeannine-time. Jeanine is neat, I suppose, but to me she looks as if she's wandering all over the place: hanging earrings, metal links for a belt, her hair escaping from a net, ruffles on her sleeves; and on that kind of shapeless, raglan-sleeved coat that always looks as if it's dragging itself off the wearer's shoulders, a pin in the shape of a crescent moon with three stars dangling from it on three fine, separate chains. Her coat and shoulder bag are overflowing into her neighbors' laps.

So I remember the horsehair petticoats of my teens, which bounded out of one's hands every time one tried to roll them or fold them up. One per drawer. The train groaned and ground to a stop somewhere between one hundred and eightieth and one hundred and sixty-eighth streets. We can look over the plain of the Bronx, which is covered with houses, to something near the river in the distance—a new stadium, I think.

Petticoats,   waist-cinchers,   boned   strapless brassières with torturous nodes where the bones began

83

or ended, modestly high-heeled shoes, double-circle skirts, felt appliquéd with sequins, bangle bracelets that always fell off, winter coats with no buttons to hold them shut, rhinestone sunburst brooches that caught on everything. Horrible obsessions, The Home, for example. We sat looking over the tenements, the faraway bridge, the ball park. There were public parks on islands in the river where I don't remember there being anything of the kind. Jeannine's giving me gooseflesh, whisper, whisper on the side of the neck (about somebody else's home permanent across the car), never still, always twisting around to look at something, forever fiddling with her clothes, suddenly deciding she just has to see out the window, I'll die if I don't. We changed places so she wouldn't have the bar between the windows cutting off her field of view. The sun shone as if on the Perfect City of my twelve-year-old dreams, the kind of thing you see on a billboard under Pittston, Future Jewel Of The Finger Lakes, the ramps, the graceful walkways, the moving belts between hundred-story buildings, the squares of green that are supposed to be parks, and above it all, in the cloudless modern sky, just one sleek, futuristic Airplane.

II

JEANNINE: Cal is too much. I don't know if I ought to give him up or not. He's awfully sweet but he's such a baby. And the cat doesn't like him, you know. He doesn't take me any place. I know he doesn't make much money, but you would think he would try, wouldn't you? All he wants is to sit around and look at me and then when we get in bed, he doesn't do anything for the longest time; that just can't be right. All he does is pet and he says he likes it like that. He says it's like floating. Then when he does *it*, you know, sometimes he cries. I never heard of a man doing that.

MYSELF: Nothing.

JEANNINE: I think there's something wrong with

him. I think he's traumatized by being so short. He wants to get married so we can have children—on his salary! When we pass a baby carriage with a baby, we both run over to look at it. He can't make up his mind, either. I never heard of a man like that. Last fall we were going to go to a Russian restaurant and I wanted to go to this place so he said all right, and then I changed my mind and wanted to go to the other place and he said OK, fine, but it turned out to be shut. So what could we do? *He* didn't know. So I lost my temper.

ME: Nothing, nothing, nothing.

SHE: He's just too much. Do you think I should get rid of him?

ME: (I shook my head)

JEANNINE (Confidingly): Well, he *is* funny sometimes.

(She bent down to pick lint off her blouse, giving herself a momentary double chin. She pursed her lips, pouted, bridled, drooped her eyelids in a knowing look.)

Sometimes—*sometimes*—he likes to get *dressed up*. He gets into the drapes like a sarong and puts on all my necklaces around his neck, and stands there with the curtain rod for a spear. He wants to be an actor, you know. But I think there's something wrong with him. Is it what they call transvestism?

JOANNA: No, Jeannine.

JEANNINE: I think it might be. I think I'll throw him over. I don't like anybody calling my cat, Mr. Frosty, names. Cal calls him The Blotchy Skinny Cat. Which he isn't. Besides, I'm going to call up my brother next week and go stay with him during vacation—I get three weeks. It gets pretty dull by the end of it—my brother stays in a small town in the Poconos, you know—but the last time I was there, there was a block dance and a Grange supper and I met a very, very handsome man. You can tell when somebody likes you, can't you? He liked me. He's an assistant to the butcher and he's going to inherit the business; he's got a real future. I went there quite a lot; I can tell, the way somebody looks at me. Mrs. Robert Poirier. Jeannine Dadier-Poirier. Ha ha! He's good-looking. Cal—

Cal is—well! Still, Cal is sweet. Poor, but sweet. I wouldn't give up Cal for anything. I enjoy being a girl, don't you? I wouldn't be a man for anything; I think they have such a hard time of it. I like being admired. I like being a girl. I wouldn't be a man for anything. Not for *anything*.

ME: Has anyone proposed the choice to you lately?

JEANNINE: I won't be a man.

ME: Nobody axed you to.

III

She was sick in the subway. Not really, but almost. She indicated by signs that she was going to be sick or had just been sick or was afraid she was going to be sick.

She held my hand.

IV

We got out at forty-second street; and this is the way things really happen, in broad daylight, publicly, invisibly; we meandered past the shops. Jeannine saw a pair of stockings that she just had to have. We went in the store and the store owner bullied us. Outside again with her stockings (wrong size) she said, "But I didn't *want* them!" They were red fishnet hose, which she'll never dare wear. In the store window there was a zany-faced mannequin who roused my active hatred: painted long ago, now dusty and full of hair-fine cracks, a small shopkeeper's economy. "Ah!" said Jeannine sorrowfully, looking again at the edge of the fishnet hose in her package. Mannequins are always dancing, this absurd throwing back of the head and

86

bending of the arms and legs. They enjoy being mannequins. (But I won't be mean.) I will not say that the
sky ripped open from top to bottom, from side to side,
that from the clouds over Fifth Avenue descended
seven angels with seven trumpets, that the vials of
wrath were loosed over Jeannine-time and the Angel of
Pestilence sank Manhattan in the deepest part of the
sea. Janet, our only savior, turned the corner in a gray
flannel jacket and a gray flannel skirt down to her
knees. That's a compromise between two worlds. She
seemed to know where she was going. Badly sun-
burned, with more freckles than usual across her flat
nose, Miss Evason stopped in the middle of the street,
scratched her head all over, yawned, and entered a
drugstore. We followed.

"I'm sorry, but I've never heard of that," said the
man behind the counter.

"Oh my goodness, really?" said Miss Evason. She
put away a piece of paper, on which she had written
whatever-it-was, and went to the other side of the store,
where she had a soda.

"You'll need a prescription," said the man behind
the counter.

"Oh my goodness," Miss Evason said mildly. It
did not help that she was carrying her soda. She put it
down on the plastic counter top and joined us at the
door, where Miss Dadier was trying—softly but very
determinedly—to bolt. She wanted to get back to the
freedom of Fifth Avenue, where there were so many
gaps—so much For Rent, so much cheaper, so much
older, than I remembered.

Miss Dadier looked sulkily up at the sky, calling
on the invisible angels and the Wrath of God to wit-
ness, and then she said, grudgingly:

"I can't *imagine* what you were trying to buy."
She did not want to admit that Janet existed. Janet
raised her eyebrows and directed a glance at me, but I
don't know. I never know anything.

"I have athlete's foot," said Miss Evason.

Jeannine shuddered. (Catch her taking off her
shoes in public!) "I thought I'd lost you."

"You didn't," said Miss Evason tolerantly. "Are you ready?"

"No," said Jeannine. But she did not repeat it. I'm not sure I'm ready. Janet led us out into the street and had us stand close together, all within one square of the sidewalk. She looked at her watch. The Whileawayan antennae come searching through the ages like a cat's whisker. It would have been better to leave from some less public spot, but they don't seem to care what they do; Janet waved engagingly at passersby and I became aware that I had become aware that I remembered becoming aware of the curved wall eighteen inches from my nose. The edge of the sidewalk, where the traffic. Had been.

Now I know how I got to Whileaway, but how did I get stuck with Jeannine? And how did Janet get into that world and not mine? Who did that? When the question is translated into Whilewayan, Dear Reader, you will see the technicians of Whileaway step back involuntarily; you will see Boy Scout Evason blanch; you will see the Chieftainess of the Whileawayan scientific establishment, mistress of ten thousand slaves and wearer of the bronze breastplates, direct stern questions right and left, while frowning. Etcetera.

Oh, oh, oh, oh, oh Jeannine was saying miserably under her breath. *I don't want to be here. They forced me. I want to go home. This is a terrible place.*

"Who did that?" said Miss Evason. "Not me. Not my people."

V

Praise God, Whose image we put in the plaza to make the eleven-year-olds laugh. She has brought me home.

VI

Dig in. Winter's coming. When I—not the "I" above but the "I" down here, naturally; that's Janet up there—

When "I" dream of Whileaway, I dream first of the farms, and although words are inadequate to this great theme, while I live I yet must tell you that the farms are the only family units on Whileaway, not because Whileawayans think farm life is good for children (they don't) but because farm work is harder to schedule and demands more day-to-day continuity than any other kind of job. Farming on Whileaway is mainly caretaking and machine-tending; it is the emotional security of family life that provides the glamor. I do not know this from observation; I know it from knowledge; I have never visited Whileaway in my own person, and when Janet, Jeannine, and Joanna stepped out of the stainless steel sphere into which they had been transported from wherever the dickens it was that they were before (etcetera), they did so alone. I was there only as the spirit or soul of an experience is always there.

Sixty eight-foot-tall Amazons, the Whileawayan Praetorian Guard, threw daggers in all directions (North, South, East, and West).

Janet, Jeannine, and Joanna arrived in the middle of a field at the end of an old-fashioned tarmac that stretched as a feeder to the nearest hovercraft highway. No winter, few roofs. Vittoria and Janet embraced and stood very still, as Aristophanes describes. They didn't yell or pound each other's shoulders, or kiss, or hug, or cry out, or jump up and down, or say "You old son-of-a-gun!" or tell each other all the news, or push each other to arm's length and screech, and then hug each other again. More farsighted than either Jeannine or Janet, I can see beyond the mountain range on the horizon, beyond the Altiplano, to the whale-herders and underground fisheries on the other side of the world; I can see desert gardens and zoological preserves; I can see storms brewing. Jeannine gulped. *Must they do that in public?* There are a few fluffy summer clouds above Green Bay, each balancing on its own tail of hot air; the dust settles on either side of the highway as a hovercar roars and passes. Vittoria's too stocky for Jeannine's taste; she could at least be good-looking. We strolled down the feeder road to the road to the hovercraft-way, observed by nobody, all alone, except that I can see a weather satellite that sees me. Jeannine keeps just behind Vittoria, staring with censorious horror at Vittoria's long, black hair.

"If they know we're here," says Jeannine, the world falling about her ears, "why didn't they send someone to meet us? I mean, other people."

"Why should they?" says Janet.

VII

JEANNINE: But we might lose our way.

JANET: You can't. I'm here and I know the way.

JEANNINE: Suppose you weren't with us. Suppose we'd killed you.

JANET: Then it would certainly be preferable that you lose your way!

JEANNINE: But suppose we held you as a hostage? Suppose you were alive but we *threatened* to kill you?

JANET: The longer it takes to get anywhere, the more time I have to think of what to do. I can probably stand thirst better than you can. And of course, since you have no map, I can mislead you and not tell you the truth about where to go.

JEANNINE: But we'd get there eventually, wouldn't we?

JANET: Yes. So there's no difference, you see.

JEANNINE: But suppose we *killed* you?

JANET: Either you killed me before you got here, in which case I am dead, or you kill me after you get

90

here, in which case I am dead. It makes no difference to me where I die.

JEANNINE: But suppose we brought a—a cannon or a bomb or something—suppose we fooled you and then seized the Government and threatened to blow everything up!

JANET: For the purposes of argument, let us suppose that. First of all, there is no government here in the sense that you mean. Second, there is no one place from which to control the entire activity of Whileaway, that is, the economy. So your one bomb isn't enough, even supposing you could kill off our welcoming committee. Introducing an entire army or an entire arsenal through the one point would take either a very advanced technology—which you have not got—or vast amounts of time. If it took you vast amounts of time, that would be no problem for us; if you came through right away, you must come through either prepared or unprepared. If you came through prepared, waiting would only assure that you spread out, used up your supplies, and acquired a false sense of confidence; if you came through unprepared and had to spend time putting things together, that would be a sign that your technology is not so advanced and you're not that much of a threat one way or the other.

JEANNINE (controlling herself): Hm!

JANET: You see, conflicts between states are not identical with conflicts between persons. You exaggerate this business of surprise. Relying on the advantage of a few hours is not a very stable way of proceeding, is it? A way of life so unprotected would hardly be worth keeping.

JEANNINE: I hope—I don't hope really because it would be awful but just to pay you out I hope!—well, I hope that some enemy with fantastically advanced technology sends experts in through that what-do-you-call-it and I hope they freeze everybody within fifty miles with *green rays*—and then I hope they make that whatever-you-call-it a *permanent* whatever-you-call-it so they can bring through *anything* they want to *whenever* they want to and *kill you all!*

JANET: Now there's an example worth talking

91

about. First, if they had a technology as advanced as that, they could open their own access points, and we certainly can't watch everywhere at all times. It would make life too obsessive. But suppose they must use this single one. No welcoming committee—or defensive army, even—could withstand those fifty-mile green rays, yes? So that's not worth sending an army against, is it? They would just be frozen or killed. However, I suspect that the use of such a fifty-mile green ray would produce all sorts of grossly observable phenomena—that is, it would be instantly obvious that something or somebody was paralyzing everything within a radius of fifty miles—and if these technologically advanced but unamiable persons were so obliging as to announce themselves in that fashion, we'd hardly need to find out about their existence by sending anyone here in the flesh, would we?

(A long silence. Jeannine is trying to think of something desperately crushing. Her platform wedgies aren't made for walking and her feet hurt.)

JANET: Besides, it's never at the first contact that these things happen. I'll show you the theory, some day.

Some day (thinks Jeannine) somebody will get you in spite of all that rationality. All that rationality will go straight up into the air. They don't have to invade; they can just blow you up from outer space; they can just infect you with plague, or infiltrate, or form a fifth column. They can corrupt you. There are all sorts of horrors. You think life is safe but it isn't, it isn't at all. It's just horrors. Horrors!

JANET (reading her face, jerking a thumb upwards from a closed fist in the Whileawayan gesture of religion): God's will be done.

VIII

Stupid and inactive. Pathetic. Cognitive starvation. Jeannine loves to become entangled with the souls of

the furniture in my apartment, softly drawing herself in
to fit inside them, pulling one long limb after another
into the cramped positions of my tables and chairs. The
dryad of my living room. I can look anywhere, at the
encyclopedia stand, at the cheap lamps, at the homey
but comfortable brown couch; it is always Jeannine
who looks back. It's uncomfortable for me but such a
relief to her. That long, young, pretty body loves to be
sat on and I think if Jeannine ever meets a Satanist, she
will find herself perfectly at home as his altar at a
Black Mass, relieved of personality at last and forever.

IX

Then there is the joviality, the self-consequence,
the forced heartiness, the benevolent teasing, the insis-
tent demands for flattery and reassurance. This is what
ethologists call dominance behavior.

EIGHTEEN-YEAR-OLD MALE COLLEGE FRESHMAN
(laying down the law at a party): If Marlowe had lived,
he would have written *very much better plays* than
Shakespeare's.

ME, A THIRTY-FIVE-YEAR-OLD PROFESSOR OF
ENGLISH (dazed with boredom): Gee, how clever you
are to know about things that never happened.

THE FRESHMAN (bewildered): Huh?

OR

EIGHTEEN-YEAR-OLD GIRL AT A PARTY: Men
don't understand machinery. The gizmo goes on the
whatsit and the rataplan makes contact with the four-
chette in at least seventy percent of all cases.

THIRTY-FIVE-YEAR-OLD MALE PROFESSOR OF
ENGINEERING (awed): Gee. (Something wrong here, I
think)

OR

"Man" is a rhetorical convenience for "human."
"Man" includes "woman." Thus:

1. The Eternal Feminine leads us ever upward
and on. (Guess who "us" is)

2. The last man on earth will spend the last hour before the holocaust searching for his wife and child. (Review of *The Second Sex* by the first sex)

3. We all have the impulse, at times, to get rid of our wives. (Irving Howe, introduction to Hardy, talking about my wife)

4. Great scientists choose their problems as they choose their wives. (A.H. Maslow, who should know better)

5. Man is a hunter who wishes to compete for the best kill and the best female. (everybody)

OR

The game is a dominance game called I Must Impress This Woman. Failure makes the active player play harder. Wear a hunched back or a withered arm; you will then experience the invisibility of the passive player. I'm never impressed—no woman ever is—it's just a cue that you like me and I'm supposed to like that. If you really like me, maybe I can get you to stop. Stop; I want to talk to you! Stop; I want to see you! Stop; I'm dying and disappearing!

SHE: Isn't it just a game?

HE: Yes, of course.

SHE: And if you play the game, it means you like me, doesn't it?

HE: Of course.

SHE: Then if it's just a game and you like me, you can stop playing. Please stop.

HE: No.

SHE: Then *I* won't play.

HE: Bitch! You want to destroy me. I'll show you. (He plays harder)

SHE: All right. I'm impressed.

HE: You really are sweet and responsive after all. You've kept your femininity. You're not one of those hysterical feminist bitches who wants to be a man and have a penis. *You're a woman*.

SHE: Yes. (She kills herself)

94

X

This book is written in blood.
Is it written entirely in blood?
No, some of it is written in tears.
Are the blood and tears all mine?

Yes, they have been in the past. But the future is a different matter. As the bear swore in *Pogo* after having endured a pot shoved on her head, being turned upside down while still in the pot, a discussion about her edibility, the lawnmowering of her behind, and a fistful of ground pepper in the snoot, she then swore a mighty oath on the ashes of her mothers (*i.e.* her forebears) grimly but quietly while the apples from the shaken apple tree above her dropped bang thud on her head:

OH, SOMEBODY ASIDES ME IS GONNA RUE THIS HERE PARTICULAR DAY.

XI

I study Vittoria's blue-black hair and velvety brown eyes, her heavy, obstinate chin. Her waist is too long (like a flexible mermaid's), her solid thighs and buttocks surprisingly sturdy. Vittoria gets a lot of praise in Whileaway because of her big behind. She is modestly interesting, like everything else in this world formed for the long acquaintance and the close view; they work outdoors in their pink or gray pajamas and indoors in the nude until you know every wrinkle and fold of flesh, until your body's in a common medium with theirs and there are no pictures made out of anybody or anything; everything becomes translated instantly into its own inside. Whileaway is the inside of everything else. I slept in the Belins' common room for three weeks, surrounded in my coming and going by people with names like Nofretari Ylayeson and Nguna Twason. (I translate freely; the names are Chinese, African, Russian, European. Also, Whileawayans love to use old names they find in dictionaries.) One little girl decided I needed a protector and stuck by me, trying to learn English. In the winter there's always heat in the kitchens for those who like the hobby of cooking and induction helmets for the little ones (to keep the heat at a distance). The Belins' kitchen was a story-telling place.

I mean, of course, that she told stories to me.

Vittoria translates, speaking softly and precisely:

"Once upon a time a long time ago there was a child who was raised by bears. Her mother went up into the woods pregnant (for there were more woods than there are today) and gave birth to the child there, for she had made an error in reckoning. Also, she had got lost. Why she was in the woods doesn't matter. It is not germane to this story.

"Well, if you must know, it was because the mother was up there to shoot bears for a zoo. She had captured three bears and shot eighteen but was running out of film; and when she went into labor, she let the three bears go, for she didn't know how long the labor would last, and there was nobody to feed the bears. They conferred with each other and stayed around, though, because they had never seen a human being give birth before and they were interested. Everything went fine until the baby's head came out, and then the Spirit of the Woods, who is very mischievous and clever, decided to have some fun. So right after the baby came out, it sent a rock slide down the mountain and the rock slide cut the umbilical cord and knocked the mother to one side. And then it made an earthquake which separated the mother and the baby by miles and miles, like the Grand Canyon in South Continent."

"Isn't that going to be a lot of trouble?" said I.

"Do you want to hear this story or don't you?" (Vittoria translated) "*I* say they were separated by miles and miles. When the mother saw this, she said

96

'Damn!' Then she went back to civilization to get a search party together, but by that time the bears had decided to adopt the baby and all of them were hidden up above. the forty-ninth parallel, where it's very rocky and wild. So the little girl grew up with the bears.

"When she was ten, there began to be trouble. She had some bear friends by then, although she didn't like to walk on all-fours as the bears did and the bears didn't like that, because bears are very conservative. She argued that walking on all-fours didn't suit her skeletal development. The bears said, 'Oh, but we have always walked this way.' They were pretty stupid. But nice, I mean. Anyway, she walked upright, the way it felt best, but when it came to copulation, that was another matter. There was nobody to copulate with. The little girl wanted to try it with her male-best-bear-friend (for animals do not live the way people do, you know) but the he-bear would not even try. 'Alas' he said (You can tell by that he was much more elegant than the other bears, ha ha) 'I'm afraid I'd hurt you with my claws because you don't have all the fur that she-bears have. And besides that, you have trouble assuming the proper position because your back legs are too long. And besides *that,* you don't smell like a bear and I'm afraid my Mother would say it was bestiality.' That's a joke. Actually it's race prejudice. The little girl was very lonely and bored. Finally after a long time, she browbeat her bear-mother into telling her about her origins, so she decided to go out looking for some people who were not bears. She thought life might be better with them. She said good-bye to her bear-friends and started South, and they all wept and waved their handkerchiefs. The girl was very hardy and woods-wise, since she had been taught by the bears. She traveled all day and slept all night. Finally she came to a settlement of people, just like this one, and they took her in. Of course she didn't speak people-talk" (with a sly glance at me) "and they didn't speak bearish. This was a big problem. Eventually she learned their language so she could talk to them and when they found out she had been raised by bears, they directed her to the Geddes Regional Park where she spent a great deal of time speaking bearish to the scholars. She made friends and so had plenty of people to copulate with, but on moonlit nights she longed to be back with the bears, for she wanted to do the great bear dances, which bears do under the full moon. So eventually she went back North again. But it turned out that the bears were a bore. So she decided to find her human mother. At the flats to Rabbit Island she found a statue with an inscription that said, 'Go that way,' so she did. At the exit from the bridge to North Continent she found an arrow sign that had been overturned, so she followed in the new direction it was pointing. The Spirit of Chance was tracking her. At the entry into Green Bay she found a huge goldfish bowl barring her way, which turned into the Spirit of Chance, a very very old woman with tiny, dried-up legs, sitting on top of a wall. The wall stretched *all* the way across the forty-eighth parallel.

" 'Play cards with me,' said the Spirit of Chance.

" 'Not on your life,' said the little girl, who was nobody's fool.

"Then the Spirit of Chance winked and said, 'Aw, come on,' so the girl thought it might be fun. She was just going to pick up her hand when she saw that the Spirit of Chance was wearing an induction helmet with a wire that stretched back way into the distance.

"She was connected with a computer!

" 'That's cheating!' cried the little girl. She ran at the wall and they had just an awful fight, but in the end everything melted away, leaving a handful of pebbles and sand, and afterward that melted away, too. The little girl walked by day and slept by night, wondering whether she would like her real mother. She didn't know if she would want to stay with her real mother or not. But when they got to know each other, they decided against it. The mother was a very smart, beautiful lady with fuzzy black hair combed out round, like electricity. But she had to go build a bridge (and fast, too) because the people couldn't get from one place to the other place without the bridge. So the little girl went to school and had lots of lovers and friends, and practiced archery, and got into a family, and had lots of adventures, and saved everybody from a volcano by bombing it from the air in a glider, and achieved Enlightenment.

"Then one morning somebody told her there was a bear looking for her—"

"Wait a minute," said I. "This story doesn't have an end. It just goes on and on. What about the volcano? And the adventures? And the achieving Enlightenment—surely that takes some time, doesn't it?"

"I tell things," said my dignified little friend (through Vittoria) "the way they happen," and slipping her head under the induction helmet without further comment (and her hands into the waldoes) she went back to stirring her blanc-mange with her forefinger. She said something casually over her shoulder to Vittoria, who translated:

"Anyone who lives in two worlds," (said Vittoria) "is bound to have a complicated life."

(I learned later that she had spent three days making up the story. It was, of course, about me).

XII

Some homes are extruded foam: white caves hung with veils of diamonds, indoor gardens, ceilings that weep. There are places in the Arctic, to sit and meditate, invisible walls that shut in the same ice as outside, the same clouds. There is one rain-forest, there is one shallow sea, there is one mountain chain, there is one desert. Human rookeries asleep undersea where Whileawayans create, in their leisurely way, a new economy and a new race. Rafts anchored in the blue eye of a dead volcano. Eyries built for nobody in particular, whose guests arrive by glider. There are many more shelters than homes, many more homes than persons; as the saying goes, My home is in my shoes. Everything (they know) is eternally in transit. Everything is pointed toward death. Radar dish-ears listen for whispers from Outside. There is no pebble, no tile, no excrement, that is not Tao; Whileaway is inhabited by the pervasive spirit of underpopulation, and alone at twilight in the permanently deserted city that is only a jungle of sculptured forms set on the Altiplano, attending to the rush of one's own breath in the respiratory mask, then—

I gambled for chores and breakfast with an old, old woman, in the middle of the night by the light of an alcohol lamp, somewhere on the back roads of the swamp and pine flats of South Continent. Watching the shadows dance on her wrinkled face, I understood why other women speak with awe of seeing the withered legs dangling from the shell of a computer housing: Humpty Dumptess on her way to the ultimate Inside of things.

(I lost. I carried her baggage and did her chores for a day.)

An ancient statue outside the fuel-alcohol distillery at Ciudad Sierra: a man seated on a stone, his knees spread, both hands pressed against the pit of his stomach, a look of blind distress, face blurred by time. Some wag has carved on the base the sideways eight that means infinity and added a straight line down from the middle; this is both the Whileaway schematic of the male genital and the mathematical symbol for self-contradiction.

If you are so foolhardy as to ask a Whileawayan child to "be a good girl" and do something for you:
"What does running other people's errands have to do with being a good girl?
"Why can't you run your own errands?
"Are you crippled?"
(The double pairs of hard, dark children's eyes everywhere, like mating cats'.)

XIII

A quiet country night. The hills East of Green
Bay, the wet heat of August during the day. One
woman reads; another sews; another smokes. Somebody takes from the wall a kind of whistle and plays on
it the four notes of the major chord. This is repeated
over and over again. We hold on to these four notes as
long as possible; then we transform them by one note;
again we repeat these four notes. Slowly something
tears itself away from the not-melody. Distances between the harmonics stretch wider and wider. No one is
dancing tonight. How the lines open up! Three notes
now. The playfulness and terror of the music written
right on the air. Although the player is employing
nearly the same dynamics throughout, the sounds have
become painfully loud; the little instrument's guts are
coming out. Too much to listen to, with its lips right
against my ear. I believe that by dawn it will stop, by
dawn we will have gone through six or seven changes
of notes, maybe two in an hour.

By dawn we'll know a little something about the
major triad. We'll have celebrated a little something.

XIV

How Whileawayans Celebrate

Dorothy Chiliason in the forest glade, her moon-
green pajamas, big eyes, big shoulders, her broad lips
and big breasts, each with its protruding thumb, her
aureole of fuzzy, ginger-colored hair. She springs to her
feet and listens. One hand up in the air, thinking. Then
both hands up. She shakes her head. She takes a glid-

101

ing step, dragging one foot. Then again. Again. She takes on some extra energy and runs a little bit. Then stops. She thinks a little bit. Whileawayan celebratory dancing is not like Eastern dancing with its motions in toward the body, its cushions of warm air exhaled by the dancer, its decorations by contradictory angles (leg up, knee down, foot up; one arm up-bent, the other arm down-bent). Nor is it at all like the yearning-for-flight of Western ballet, limbs shooting out in heaven-aspiring curves, the torso a mathematical point. If Indian dancing says I Am, if ballet says I Wish, what does the dance of Whileaway say?

It says I Guess. (The intellectuality of this impossible business!)

XV

What Whileawayans Celebrate

The full moon
The Winter solstice (You haven't lived if you haven't seen us running around in our skivvies, banging on pots and pans, shouting "Come back, sun! Goddammit, come back! Come back!")
The Summer solstice (rather different)
The autumnal equinox
The vernal equinox
The flowering of trees
The flowering of bushes
The planting of seeds
Happy copulation
Unhappy copulation
Longing
Jokes
Leaves falling off the trees (where deciduous)
Acquiring new shoes
Wearing same
Birth

The contemplation of a work of art
Marriages
Sport
Divorces
Anything at all
Nothing at all
Great ideas
Death

XVI

There is an unpolished, white, marble statue of God on Rabbit Island, all alone in a field of weeds and snow. She is seated, naked to the waist, an outsized female figure as awful as Zeus, her dead eyes staring into nothing. At first She is majestic; then I notice that Her cheekbones are too broad, Her eyes set at different levels, that Her whole figure is a jumble of badly-matching planes, a mass of inhuman contradictions. There is a distinct resemblance to Dunyasha Bernadetteson, known as The Playful Philosopher (A.C. 344–426), though God is older than Bernadetteson and it's possible that Dunyasha's genetic surgeon modelled her after God instead of the other way round. Persons who look at the statue longer than I did have reported that one cannot pin It down at all, that She is a constantly changing contradiction, that She becomes in turn gentle, terrifying, hateful, loving, "stupid" (or "dead") and finally indescribable.

Persons who look at Her longer than that have been known to vanish right off the face of the Earth.

XVII

I have never been to Whileaway.
Whileawayans breed into themselves an immunity

to ticks, mosquitoes, and other insect parasites. I have none. And the way into Whileaway is barred neither by time, distance, nor an angel with a flaming sword, but by a cloud or crowd of gnats.

Talking gnats.

PART SIX

I

Jeannine wakes from a dream of Whileaway. She has to go to her brother's this week. Everything suggests to Jeannine something she has lost, although she doesn't put it to herself this way; what she understands is that everything in the world wears a faint coating of nostalgia, makes her cry, seems to say to her, "You can't." She's fond of not being able to do things; somehow this gives her a right to something. Her eyes fill with tears. Everything's a cheat. If she gets up right now, she'll be able to make the early bus; she also wants to get away from the dream that still lingers in the folds of her bedclothes, in the summery smell of her soft old sheets, a smell of herself that Jeannine likes but wouldn't admit to anybody. The bed is full of dreamy, suspicious hollows. Jeannine yawns, out of a sense of duty. She gets up and makes the bed, then picks paperback books up off the floor (murder mysteries) and puts them away in her bookcase. There are clothes to wash before she goes, clothes to put away, stockings to pair and put in the drawers. She wraps the garbage in newspaper and carries it down three flights to put it in the garbage can. She routs Cal's socks from behind the bed and shakes them out, leaving them on the kitchen table. There are dishes to wash, soot on the window sills, soaking pots to scour, a dish to put under the radiator in case it goes on during the week (it leaks). Oh. Ugh. Let the windows go, though Cal doesn't like them dirty. That awful job of scrubbing out the toilet, whisk-brooming the furniture. Clothes to iron. Things always fall off when you straighten other things. She bends and bends. Flour and sugar spill on the shelves over the sink and have to be mopped up; there are stains and spills, rotting radish leaves, and encrustations of ice inside the old refrigerator (it has to be propped open with a chair to defrost itself). Odds and ends of paper, candy, cigarettes, cigarette ashes all over the room. Everything has to be dusted. She decides to do the windows anyway, because it's nice. They'll be filthy in a week. Of course nobody else helps. Nothing is the right height. She adds Cal's socks to her clothes and his clothes that she has to take to the self-service laundry, makes a separate pile of his clothes that have to be mended, and sets the table for herself. She scrapes old food from her cat's dish into the garbage, washes the dish, and sets out new water and milk. Mr. Frosty doesn't seem to be around. Under the sink Jeannine finds a dishcloth, hangs it up over the sink, reminds herself to clean out under there later, and pours out cold cereal, tea, toast, orange juice. (The orange juice is a government package of powdered orange-and-grapefruit and tastes awful.) She jumps up to rummage around for the mop head under the sink, and the galvanized pail, also somewhere down in there. Time to mop the bathroom floor and the square of linoleum in front of the sink and stove. First she finishes her tea, leaves half the orange-and-grapefruit juice (making a face) and some of the cereal. Milk goes back in the refrigerator—no, wait a minute, throw it out— she sits down for a moment and writes out a list of groceries to buy on the way back from the bus in a week. Fill the pail, find the soap, give up, mop it anyway with just water. Put everything away. Do the breakfast dishes. She picks up a murder mystery and sits on the couch, riffling through it. Jump up, wash the table, pick up the salt that falls on the rug and brush it up with the whisk-broom. Is that all? No, mend Cal's clothes and her own. Oh, let them be. She has to pack and make her lunch and Cal's (although he's not going with her). That means things coming out of the icebox again and mopping the table again—leaving footprints on the linoleum again. Well, it doesn't matter. Wash the knife

106

and the plate. Done. She decides to go get the sewing box to do his clothes, then changes her mind. Instead she picks up the murder mystery. *Cal will say, "You didn't sew my clothes."* She goes to get the sewing box out of the back of the closet, stepping over her valises, boxes of stuff, the ironing board, her winter coat and winter clothes. Little hands reach out of Jeannine's back and pick up what she drops. She sits on her couch, fixing the rip in his summer suit jacket, biting off the thread with her front teeth. *You'll chip the enamel.* Buttons. Mending three socks. (The others seem all right.) Rubbing the small of her back. Fastening the lining of a skirt where it's torn. Inspecting her stockings for runs. Polishing shoes. She pauses and looks at nothing. Then she shakes herself and with an air of extraordinary energy gets her middling-sized valise from the closet and starts laying out her clothes for the week. *Cal won't let me smoke. He really cares about me.* With everything cleaned up, she sits and looks at her room. The *Post* says you should get cobwebs off the ceiling with a rag tied to a broom handle. *Well, I can't see them.* Jeannine wishes for the she-doesn't-know-how-many-times time that she had a real apartment with more than one room, though to decorate it properly would be more than she could afford. There's a pile of home-decorating magazines in the back of the closet, although that was only a temporary thing; the thought doesn't really recur to her much. Cal doesn't understand about such things. *Tall, dark, and handsome.... She refused her lover.... the noble thing to.... mimosa and jasmine....* She thinks how it would be to be a mermaid and decorate a merhouse with seaweed and slices of pearl. *The Mermaid's Companion. The Mermaid's Home Journal.* She giggles. She finishes packing her clothes, taking out a pair of shoes to polish them with a bottle of neutral polish, because you have to be careful with the light colors. As soon as they dry, they'll go back in the valise. Trouble is, though, the valise is bloody well falling apart at the seams. Cal, when he comes, will find her reading *Mademoiselle Mermaid* about the new fish-scale look for eyes.

Why does she keep having these dreams about Whileaway?

While-away. While. A. Way. To While away the time. That means it's just a pastime. If she tells Cal about it, he'll say she's nattering again; worse still, it *would* sound pretty silly; you can't expect a man to listen to everything (as everybody's Mother said). Jeannine gets dressed in blouse, sweater, and skirt for her brother's place in the country, while in the valise she puts: a pair of slacks to go berrying in, another blouse, a scarf, underwear, stockings, a jacket *(No, I'll carry it)*, her hairbrush, her makeup, face cream, sanitary napkins, a raincoat, jewelry for the good dress, hair clips, hair curlers, bathing suit, and a light every-day dress. Oof, too heavy! She sits down again, discouraged. Little things make Jeannine blue. What's the use of cleaning a place over and over again if you can't make something of it? The ailanthus tree nods to her from outside the window. (And why won't Cal protect her against anything? She deserves protection.) Maybe she'll meet somebody. Nobody knows—O nobody knows really—what's in Jeannine's heart (she thinks). But somebody will see. Somebody will understand. Remember the hours in California under the fig tree. Jeannine in her crisp plaid dress, the hint of fall in the air, the blue haze over the hills like smoke. She hauls at the valise again, wondering desperately what it is that other women know and can do that she doesn't know or can't do, women in the street, women in the magazines, the ads, married women. Why life doesn't match the stories. *I ought to get married.* (But not to Cal!) She'll meet someone on the bus; she'll sit next to someone. Who knows why things happen? Jeannine, who sometimes believes in astrology, in palmistry, in occult signs, who knows that certain things are fated or not fated, knows that men—in spite of everything—have no contact with or understanding of the insides of things. That's a realm that's denied them. Women's magic, women's intuition rule here, the subtle deftness forbidden to the clumsier sex. Jeannine is on very good terms with her ailanthus tree. Without having to reflect on it, without having to work at it, they both bring into human life the breath of magic and desire. They merely embody. Mr. Frosty, knowing he's going to be left at a neighbor's for the week, has been hiding behind the couch; now he crawls out with a piece of dust stuck on his left eye-tuft, looking very miserable. Jeannine has no idea what drove him out. "Bad cat!" *There was something about her.* She watches the blotchy-skinny-cat (as Cal calls him) sneak to his milk dish and while Mr. Frosty laps it up, Jeannine grabs him. She gets the collar around his neck while Mr. Frosty struggles indignantly, and then she snaps the leash on. In a few minutes he'll forget he's confined. He'll take the collar for granted and start daydreaming about sumptuous mice. *There was something unforgettable about her....* She ties him to a bed post and pauses, catching sight of herself in the wall mirror: flushed, eyes sparkling, her hair swept back as if by some tumultuous storm, her whole face glowing. The lines of her figure are perfect, but who is to use all this loveliness, who is to recognize it, make it public, make it available? Jeannine is not available to Jeannine. She throws her jacket over one arm, more depressed than otherwise. *I wish I had money. . . .* "Don't worry," she tells the cat. "Somebody's coming for you." She arranges her jacket, her valise, and her pocketbook, and turns off the light, shutting the door behind her (it latches itself). *If only* (she thinks) *he'll come and show me to myself.*

I've been waiting for you so long. How much longer must I wait?

Nights and nights alone. ("You can't," says the stairwell. "You can't," says the street.) A fragment of old song drifts through her mind and lingers behind her in the stairwell, her thoughts lingering there, too, wishing that she could be a mermaid and float instead of walk, that she were someone else and so could watch herself coming down the stairs, the beautiful girl who composes everything around her to harmony:

Somebody lovely has just passed by.

II

I live between worlds. Half the time I like doing housework, I care a lot about how I look, I warm up to men and flirt beautifully (I mean I really admire them, though I'd die before I took the initiative; that's men's business), I don't press my point in conversations, and I enjoy cooking. I like to do things for other people, especially male people. I sleep well, wake up on the dot, and don't dream. There's only one thing wrong with me:

I'm frigid.

In my other incarnation I live out such a plethora of conflict that you wouldn't think I'd survive, would you, but I do; I wake up enraged, go to sleep in numbed despair, face what I know perfectly well is condescension and abstract contempt, get into quarrels, shout, fret about people I don't even know, live as if I were the only woman in the world trying to buck it all, work like a pig, strew my whole apartment with notes, articles, manuscripts, books, get frowsty, don't care, become stridently contentious, sometimes laugh and weep within five minutes together out of pure frustration. It takes me two hours to get to sleep and an hour to wake up. I dream at my desk. I dream all over the place. I'm very badly dressed.

But O how I relish my victuals! And O how I fuck!

III

Jeannine has an older brother who's a mathematics teacher in a New York high school. Their mother, who stays with him during vacations, was widowed when Jeannine was four. When she was a little baby

Jeannine used to practice talking; she would get into a corner by herself and say words over and over again to get them right. Her first full sentence was, "See the moon." She pressed wildflowers and wrote poems in elementary school. Jeannine's brother, her sister-in-law, their two children, and her mother live for the summer in two cottages near a lake. Jeannine will stay in the smaller one with her mother. She comes downstairs with me behind her to find Mrs. Dadier arranging flowers in a pickle jar on the kitchenette table. I am behind Jeannine, but Jeannine can't see me, of course.

"Everyone's asking about you," says Mrs. Dadier, giving her daughter a peck on the cheek.

"Mm," says Jeannine, still sleepy. I duck behind the bookshelves that separate the living room from the kitchenette.

"We thought you might bring that nice young man with you again," says Mrs. Dadier, setting cereal and milk in front of her daughter. Jeannine retreats into sulky impassivity. I make an awful face, which of course nobody sees.

"We've separated," says Jeannine, untruly.

"Why?" says Mrs. Dadier, her blue eyes opening wide. "What was the matter with him?"

He was impotent, mother. Now how could I say that to such a nice lady? I didn't.

"Nothing," says Jeannine. "Where's Bro?"

"Fishing," says Mrs. Dadier. Brother often goes out in the early morning and meditates over a fishing line. The ladies don't. Mrs. Dadier is afraid of his slipping, falling on a rock, and splitting open his head. Jeannine doesn't like fishing.

"We're going to have a nice day," says Mrs. Dadier. "There's a play tonight and a block dance. There are lots of young people, Jeannine." With her perpetually fresh smile Mrs. Dadier clears off the table where her daughter-in-law and the two children have breakfasted earlier; Eileen has her hands full with the children.

"*Don't*, mother," says Jeannine, looking down.

"I don't mind," says Mrs. Dadier. "Bless you, I've done it often enough." Listless Jeannine pushes her

111

chair back from the table. "You haven't finished," observes Mrs. Dadier, mildly surprised. We. have to get out of here. "Well, I don't—I want to find Bro," says Jeannine, edging out, "I'll see you," and she's gone. Mrs. Dadier doesn't smile when there's nobody there. Mother and daughter wear the same face at times like that—calm and deathly tired—Jeannine idly pulling the heads off weeds at the side of the path with an abstract viciousness completely unconnected with anything going on in her head. Mrs. Dadier finishes the dishes and sighs. That's done. Always to do again. Jeannine comes to the path around the lake, the great vacation feature of the community, and starts round it, but there seems to be nobody nearby. She had hoped she would find her brother, who was always her favorite. ("My big brother") She sits on the rock by the side of the path, Jeannine the baby. Out in the lake there's a single canoe with two people in it; Jeannine's gaze, vaguely resentful, fastens on it for a moment, and then drifts off. Her sister-in-law is worried sick about one of the children; one of those children always has something. Jeannine bangs her knuckles idly on the rock. She's too sour for a romantic reverie and soon she gets up and walks on. Whoever comes to the lake anyway? Maybe Bro is at home. She retraces her steps and takes a fork off the main path, idling along until the lake, with its crowded fringe of trees and brush, disappears behind her. Eileen Dadier's youngest, the little girl, appears at the upstairs window for a moment and then vanishes. Bro is behind the cottage, cleaning fish, protecting his sports clothes with a rubber lab apron.

"Kiss me," says Jeannine. "O.K.?" She leans forward with her arms pulled back to avoid getting fish scales on herself, one cheek offered invitingly. Her brother kisses her. Eileen appears around the corner of the house, leading the boy. "Kiss Auntie," she says. "I'm so *glad* to see you, Jeannie."

"Jeannine," says Jeannine (automatically).

"Just think, Bud," says Eileen. "She must have got in last night. Did you get in last night?" Jeannine nods. Jeannine's nephew, who doesn't like anyone but his father, is pulling furiously at Eileen Dadier's hand, trying seriously to get his fingers out of hers. Bud finishes cleaning the fish. He wipes his hands methodically on a dish towel which Eileen will have to wash by hand to avoid contaminating her laundry, takes off his coat, and takes his knife and cleaver into the house, from whence comes the sound of running water. He comes out again, drying his hands on a towel.

"Oh, baby," says Eileen Dadier reproachfully to her son, "be nice to Auntie." Jeannine's brother takes his son's hand from his wife. The little boy immediately stops wriggling.

"Jeannie," he says. "It's nice to see you.

"When did you get in?

"When are you going to get married?"

IV

I found Jeannine on the clubhouse porch that evening, looking at the moon. She had run away from her family.

"They only want what's good for you," I said.

She made a face.

"They love you," I said.

A low, strangled sound. She was prodding the porch-rail with her hand.

"I think you ought to go and rejoin them, Jeannine," I said. "Your mother's a wonderful woman who has never raised her voice in anger all the time you've known her. And she brought all of you up and got you all through high school, even though she had to work. Your brother's a firm, steady man who makes a good living for his wife and children, and Eileen wants nothing more in the world than her husband and her little boy and girl. You ought to appreciate them more, Jeannine."

"I know," said Jeannine softly and precisely. Or perhaps she said *Oh no*.

"Jeannine, you'll never get a good job," I said. "There aren't any now. And if there were, they'd never give them to a woman, let alone a grown-up baby like you. Do you think you could hold down a really good job, even if you could get one? They're all boring anyway, hard and boring. You don't want to be a dried-up old spinster at forty but that's what you will be if you go on like this. You're twenty-nine. You're getting old. You ought to marry someone who can take care of you, Jeannine."

"Don't care," said she. Or was it *Not fair?*

"Marry someone who can take care of you," I went on, for her own good. "It's all right to do that; you're a girl. Find somebody like Bud who has a good job, somebody you can respect; marry him. There's no other life for a woman, Jeannine; do you want never to have children? Never to have a husband? Never to have a house of your own?" (Brief flash of waxed floor, wife in organdie apron, smiling possessively, husband with roses. That's hers, not mine.)

"Not Cal." *Ah, hell.*

"Now, really, what are you waiting for?" (I was getting impatient.) "Here's Eileen married, and here's your mother with two children, and all your old school friends, and enough couples here around the lake to fill it up if they all jumped into it at once; do you think you're any different? Fancy Jeannine! Refined Jeannine! What do you think you're waiting for?"

"For a man," said Jeannine. *For a plan.* My impression that somebody else had been echoing her was confirmed by a brief cough behind me after these words. But it turned out to be Mr. Dadier, come out to fetch his sister. He took her by the arm and pulled her toward the door. "Come on, Jeannie. We're going to introduce you to someone."

Only the woman revealed under the light was not Jeannine. A passerby inside saw the substitution through the doorway and gaped. Nobody else seemed to notice. Jeannine is still meditating by the rail: doctor, lawyer, Indian chief, poor man, rich man; maybe he'll be tall; maybe he'll make twenty thou a year; maybe he'll speak three languages and be really sophisticated, maybe. Mister Destiny. Janet, who has none of our notion that a good, dignified, ladylike look will re-

call the worst of scoundrels to a shrinking consciousness of his having insulted A Lady (that's the general
idea, anyway), has gotten out of Bud Dadier's hold by
twisting his thumb. She is the victim of a natural, but
ignorant and unjustified alarm; she thinks that being
grabbed is not just a gesture but is altogether out of
line. Janet's prepared for blue murder.

"Huh," says Bro. He's about to expostulate. "What
are you doing here? Who are you?"

Touch me again and I'll knock your teeth out!

You can see the blood rush to his face, even in
this bad light. That's what comes of being misunder-
stood. "Keep a civil tongue in your mouth, young
lady!"

Janet jeers.

"You just—" Bud Dadier begins, but Janet antici-
pates him by vanishing like a soap bubble. What do
you think Bud stands for—Buddington? Budworthy?
Or "Bud" as in "friend"? He passes his hands over his
face—the only thing left of Janet is a raucous screech
of triumph which nobody else (except the two of us)
can hear. The woman in front of the door is Jeannine.
Bro, scared out of his wits, as who wouldn't be, grabs
her.

"Oh, Bro!" says Jeannine reproachfully, rubbing
her arm.

"You oughtn't to be out here alone," says he. "It
looks as if you're not enjoying yourself. Mother went to
great trouble to get that extra ticket, you know."

"I'm sorry," says Jeannine penitently. "I just
wanted to see the moon."

"Well, you've seen it," says her brother. "You've
been out here for fifteen minutes. I ought to tell you,
Jeannie, Eileen and Mother and I have been talking
about you and we all think that you've got to do something with your life. You can't just go on drifting like
this. You're not twenty any more, you know."

"Oh, Bro—" says Jeannine unhappily. Why are
women so unreasonable? "Of course I want to have a
good time," she says.

"Then come inside and have one." (He straightens
his shirt collar.) "You might meet someone, if that's

what you want to do, and you say that's what you want."

"I do," says Jeannine. *You too?*

"Then act like it, for Heaven's sake. If you don't do it soon, you may not have another chance. Now come on." There are girls with nice brothers and girls with nasty brothers; there was a girl friend of mine who had a strikingly handsome older brother who could lift armchairs by one leg only. I was on a double date once with the two of them and another boy, and my girl friend's brother indicated the camp counselors' cottages. "Do you know what those are?

"Menopause Alley!"

We all laughed. I didn't like it, but not because it was in bad taste. As you have probably concluded by this point (correctly) I don't have any taste; that is, I don't know what bad and good taste are. I laughed because I knew I would have an awful fight on my hands if I didn't. If you don't like things like that, you're a prude. Drooping like a slave-girl, Jeannine followed Bro into the clubhouse. If only older brothers could be regularized somehow, so that one knew what to expect! If only all older brothers were younger brothers. "Well, who shall I marry?" said Jeannine, trying to make it into a joke as they entered the building. He said, with complete seriousness:

"Anybody."

V

The Great Happiness Contest

(this happens a lot)

FIRST WOMAN: I'm perfectly happy. I love my husband and we have two darling children. I certainly don't need any change in *my* lot.

SECOND WOMAN: I'm even happier than you are. My husband does the dishes every Wednesday and we have three darling children, each nicer than the last. I'm tremendously happy.

THIRD WOMAN: Neither of you is as happy as I am. I'm fantastically happy. My husband hasn't looked at another woman in the fifteen years we've been married, he helps around the house whenever I ask it, and he wouldn't mind in the least if I were to go out and get a job. But I'm happiest in fulfilling my responsibilities to him and the children. We have four children.

FOURTH WOMAN: We have *six* children. (This is too many. A long silence.) I have a part-time job as a clerk in Bloomingdale's to pay for the children's skiing lessons, but I really feel I'm expressing myself best when I make a custard or a meringue or decorate the basement.

ME: You miserable nits, I have a Nobel Peace Prize, fourteen published novels, six lovers, a town house, a box at the Metropolitan Opera, I fly a plane, I fix my own car, and I can do eighteen push-ups before breakfast, that is, if you're interested in numbers.

ALL THE WOMEN: Kill, kill, kill, kill, kill, kill.

OR, FOR STARTERS

HE: I can't stand stupid, vulgar women who read Love Comix and have no intellectual interests.

ME: Oh my, neither can I.

HE: I really admire refined, cultivated, charming women who have careers.

ME: Oh my, so do I.

HE: Why do you think those awful, stupid, vulgar, commonplace women get so awful?

ME: Well, probably, not wishing to give any offense and after considered judgment and all that, and *very* tentatively, with the hope that you won't jump on me—I think it's at least partly your fault.

(Long silence)

HE: You know, on second thought, I think bitchy, castrating, unattractive, neurotic women are even worse. Besides, you're showing your age. And your figure's going.

OR

HE: Darling, why must you work part-time as a rug salesman?

117

SHE: Because I wish to enter the marketplace and prove that in spite of my sex I can take a fruitful part in the life of the community and earn what our culture proposes as the sign and symbol of adult independence—namely money.

HE: But darling, by the time we deduct the cost of a baby-sitter and nursery school, a higher tax bracket, and your box lunches from your pay, it actually costs us money for you to work. So you see, you aren't making money at all. You can't make money. Only I can make money. Stop working.

SHE: I won't. And I hate you.

HE: But darling, why be irrational? It doesn't matter that you can't make money because *I* can make money. And after I've made it, I give it to you, because I love you. So you don't *have* to make money. Aren't you glad?

SHE: No. Why can't you stay home and take care of the baby? Why can't we deduct all those things from your pay? Why should I be glad because I can't earn a living? Why—

HE (with dignity): This argument is becoming degraded and ridiculous. I will leave you alone until loneliness, dependence, and a consciousness that I am very much displeased once again turn you into the sweet girl I married. There is no use in arguing with a woman.

OR, LAST OF ALL

HE: Is your dog drinking *cold fountain water?*

SHE: I guess so.

HE: If your dog drinks cold water, he'll get colic.

SHE: It's a she. And I don't care about the colic. You know, what I really worry about is bringing her out in public when she's in heat like this. I'm not afraid she'll get colic, but that she might get pregnant.

HE: They're the same thing, aren't they? Har har har.

SHE: Maybe for your mother they were.

(At this point Joanna the Grate swoops down on bat's wings, lays He low with one mighty swatt, and elevates She and Dog to the constellation of Victoria Femina, where they sparkle forever.)

I know that somewhere, just to give me the lie, lives a beautiful (got to be beautiful), intellectual, gracious, cultivated, charming woman who has eight children, bakes her own bread, cakes, and pies, takes care of her own house, does her own cooking, brings up her own children, holds down a demanding nine-to-five job at the top decision-making level in a man's field, and is adored by her equally successful husband because although a hard-driving, aggressive business executive with eye of eagle, heart of lion, tongue of adder, and muscles of gorilla (she looks just like Kirk Douglas), she comes home at night, slips into a filmy negligée and a wig, and turns instanter into a *Playboy* dimwit, thus laughingly dispelling the canard that you cannot be eight people simultaneously with two different sets of values. *She has not lost her femininity.*

And I'm Marie of Rumania.

VI

Jeannine is going to put on her Mommy's shoes. That caretaker of childhood and feminine companion of men is waiting for her at the end of the road we all must travel. She swam, went for walks, went to dances, had a picnic with another girl; she got books from town; newspapers for her brother, murder mysteries for Mrs. Dadier, and nothing for herself. At twenty-nine you can't waste your time reading. Either they're too young or they're married or they're bad-looking or there's something awful about them. Rejects. Jeannine went out a couple of times with the son of a friend of her mother's and tried to make conversation with him; she decided that he wasn't really so bad-looking, if only he'd talk more. They went canoeing in the middle of the lake one day and he said:

"I have to tell you something, Jeannine."

She thought: *This is it,* and her stomach knotted up.

"I'm married," he said, taking off his glasses, "but my wife and I are separated. She's living with her mother in California. She's emotionally disturbed."

"Oh," Jeannine said, flustered and not knowing what to say. She hadn't liked him particularly, but the disappointment was very bad. There is some barrier between Jeannine and real life which can be removed only by a man or by marriage; somehow Jeannine is not in touch with what everybody knows to be real life. He blinked at her with his naked eyes and oh lord, he was fat and plain; but Jeannine managed to smile. She didn't want to hurt his feelings.

"I knew you'd understand," he said in a choked voice, nearly crying. He pressed her hand. "I knew you'd understand, Jeannie." She began reckoning him up again, that swift calculation that was quite automatic by now: the looks, the job, whether he was "romantic," did he read poetry? whether he could be made to dress better or diet or put on weight (whichever it was), whether his hair could be cut better. She could make herself feel something about him, yes. She could rely on him. After all, his wife might divorce him. He was intelligent. He was promising. "I understand," she said, against the grain. After all, there wasn't anything wrong with him exactly; from shore it must really look quite good, the canoe, the pretty girl, the puffy summer clouds, Jeannine's sun-shade (borrowed from the girl friend she'd had the picnic with). There couldn't be that much wrong with it. She smiled a little. His contribution is *Make me feel good;* her contribution is *Make me exist.* The sun came out over the water and it really was quite nice. And there was this painful stirring of feeling in her, this terrible tenderness or need, so perhaps she was beginning to love him, in her own way.

"Are you busy tonight?" Poor man. She wet her lips and didn't answer, feeling the sun strike her on all sides, deliciously aware of her bare arms and neck, the picture she made. "Mm?" she said.

"I thought—I thought you might want to go to the play." He took out his handkerchief and wiped his face with it. He put his glasses back on.

"You ought to wear sunglasses," said Jeannine, imagining how he might look that way. "Yes, Bud and Eileen were going. Would you like to join us?" The surprised gratitude of a man reprieved. *I really do like him.* He bent closer—this alarmed her for the canoe, as well as disgusted her (Freud says disgust is a prominent expression of the sexual life in civilized people) and she cried out, "Don't! We'll fall in!" He righted himself. *By degrees. You've got to get to know people.* She was frightened, almost, by the access of being that came to her from him, frightened at the richness of the whole scene, at how much she felt without feeling it for him, terrified lest the sun might go behind a cloud and withdraw everything from her again.

"What time shall I pick you up?" he said.

VII

That night Jeannine fell in love with an actor. The theatre was a squat, low building finished in pink stucco like a summertime movie palace and built in the middle of a grove of pine trees. The audience sat on hard wooden chairs and watched a college group play "Charley's Aunt." Jeannine didn't get up or go out during the intermission but only sat, stupefied, fanning herself with her program and wishing that she had the courage to make some sort of change in her life. She couldn't take her eyes off the stage. The presence of her brother and sister-in-law irked her unbearably and every time she became aware of her date by her elbow, she wanted to turn in on herself and disappear, or run outside, or scream. It didn't matter which actor or which character she fell in love with; even Jeannine knew that; it was the unreality of the scene onstage that made her long to be in it or on it or two-dimensional, anything to quiet her unstable heart; *I'm not fit to live,* she said. There was more pain in it than pleasure; it had been getting worse for some years, until Jeannine now dreaded doing it; *I can't help it,* she said. She added, *I'm not fit to exist.*

I'll feel better tomorrow. She thought of Bud taking his little girl fishing (that had happened that morn-

121

ing, over Eileen's protests) and tears rose in her eyes. The pain of it. The painful pleasure. She saw, through a haze of distress, the one figure on stage who mattered to her. She willed it so. Roses and raptures in the dark. She was terrified of the moment when the curtain would fall—in love as *in* pain, *in* misery, *in* trouble. If only you could stay half-dead. Eventually the curtain (a gray velvet one, much worn) did close, and opened again on the troupe's curtain calls; Jeannine mumbled something about it being too hot and ran outside, shaking with terror; who am I, what am I, what do I want, where do I go, what world is this? One of the neighborhood children was selling lemonade, with a table and chairs pitched on the carpet of dead pine needles under the trees. Jeannine bought some, to color her loneliness; I did, too, and it was awful stuff. *(If anybody finds me, I'll say it was too warm and I wanted a drink.)* She walked blindly into the woods and stood a little way from the theatre, leaning her forehead against a tree-trunk. I said Jeannine, why are you unhappy?

I'm not unhappy.

You have everything (I said). What is there that you want and haven't got?

I want to die.

Do you want to be an airline pilot? Is that it? And they won't let you? Did you have a talent for mathematics, which they squelched? Did they refuse to let you be a truck driver? What is it?

I want to live.

I will leave you and your imaginary distresses (said I) and go converse with somebody who makes more sense; really, one would think you'd been balked of some vital necessity. Money? You've got a job. Love? You've been going out with boys since you were thirteen.

I know.

You can't expect romance to last your life long, Jeannine: candlelight dinners and dances and pretty clothes are nice but they aren't the whole of life. There comes a time when one has to live the ordinary side of life and romance is a very small part of that. No matter how nice it is to be courted and taken out, even-

tually you say "I do" and that's that. It may be a
great adventure, but there are fifty or sixty years to fill
up afterwards. You can't do that with romance alone,
you know. Think, Jeannine—fifty or sixty years!

I know.

Well?

(Silence)

Well, what do you want?

(She didn't answer)

I'm trying to talk to you sensibly, Jeannine. You
say you don't want a profession and you don't want a
man—in fact, you just fell in love but you condemn
that as silly—so what is it that you want? Well?

Nothing.

That's not true, dear. Tell me what you want.
Come on.

I want love. (She dropped her paper cup of lemonade and covered her face with her hands.)

Go ahead. The world's full of people.

I can't.

Can't? Why not? You've got a date here tonight,
haven't you? You've never had trouble attracting men's
interest before. So go to it.

Not that way.

"What way?" (said I).

Not the real way.

"What!" (said I).

I want something else, she repeated, *something
else.*

"Well, Jeannine," said I, "if you don't like reality
and human nature, I don't know what else you *can*
have," and I quit her and left her standing on the pine
needles in the shadow cast by the trees, away from the
crowd and the flood-lights fastened to the outside of the
theatre building. Jeannine is very romantic. She's
building a whole philosophy from the cry of the crick-
ets and her heart's anguish. But that won't last. She will
slowly come back to herself. She'll return to Bud and
Eileen and her job of fascinating the latest X. Jeannine,
back in the theatre building with Bud and Eileen,
looked in the mirror set up over the ticket window so

123

lady spectators could put on their lipstick, and jumped—"Who's that!"

"Stop it, Jeannie," said Bud. "What's the matter with you?" We all looked and it was Jeannine herself, sure enough, the same graceful slouch and thin figure, the same nervous, oblique glance.

"Why, it's you, darling," said Eileen, laughing. Jeannine had been shocked right out of her sorrow. She turned to her sister-in-law and said, with unwonted energy, between her teeth: "What do you want out of life, Eileen? Tell me!"

"Oh honey," said Eileen, "what should I want? I want just what I've got." X came out of the men's room. Poor fellow. Poor lay figure.

"Jeannie wants to know what life is all about," said Bud. "What do you think, Frank? Do you have any words of wisdom for us?"

"I think that you are all awful," said Jeannine vehemently. X laughed nervously. "Well now, I don't know," he said.

That's my trouble, too. My knowledge was taken away from me.

(She remembered the actor in the play and her throat constricted. It hurt, it hurt. Nobody saw, though.)

"Do you think," she said very low, to X, "that you could know what you wanted, only after a while—I mean, they don't mean to do it, but life—people—people could confuse things?"

"I know what I want," said Eileen brightly. "I want to go home and take the baby from Mama. Okay, honey?"

"I don't mean—" Jeannine began.

"Oh, Jeannie!" said Eileen affectionately, possibly more for X's benefit than her sister-in-law's; "Oh, Jeannie!" and kissed her. Bud gave her a peck on the cheek.

Don't you touch me!

"Want a drink?" said X, when Bud and Eileen had gone.

"I want to know," said Jeannine, almost under her

124

breath, "what you want out of life and I'm not moving until you tell me." He stared.

"Come on," she said. He smiled nervously.

"Well, I'm going to night school. I'm going to finish my B.A. this winter." (He's going to night school. He's going to finish his B.A. Wowie zowie. I'm not impressed.)

"Really?" said Jeannine, in real awe.

"Really," he said. Score one. That radiant look of gratitude. Maybe she'll react the same way when he tells her he can ski. In this loveliest and neatest of social interactions, she admires him, he's pleased with her admiration, this pleasure lends him warmth and style, he relaxes, he genuinely likes Jeannine; Jeannine sees this and something stirs, something hopes afresh. Is he The One? Can he Change Her Life? (Do you know what you want? No. Then don't complain.) Fleeing from the unspeakableness of her own wishes—for what happens when you find out you want something that doesn't exist?—Jeannine lands in the lap of the possible. A drowning woman, she takes X's willing, merman hands; maybe it's wanting to get married, maybe she's just waited too long. *There's* love; *there's* joy—in marriage, and you must take your chances as they come. They say life without love does strange things to you; maybe you begin to doubt love's existence.

I shouted at her and beat her on the back and on the head; oh I was an enraged and evil spirit there in the theatre lobby, but she continued holding poor X by the hands—little did he know what hopes hung on him as she continued (I say) to hold on to his hands and look into his flattered eyes. Little did she know that he was a water-dweller and would drown her. Little did she know that there was, attached to his back, a drowning-machine issued him in his teens along with his pipe and his tweeds and his ambition and his profession and his father's mannerisms. Somewhere is The One. The solution. Fulfillment. Fulfilled women. Filled full. My Prince. Come. Come away, Death. She stumbles into her Mommy's shoes, little girl playing house. I could kick her. And X thinks, poor, deceived bastard, that it's a tribute to him, of all people—as if he had any-

thing to do with it! (I still don't know whom she saw
or thought she saw in the mirror. Was it Janet? Me?)
I want to get married.

VIII

Men succeed. Women get married.
Men fail. Women get married.
Men enter monasteries. Women get married.
Men start wars. Women get married.
Men stop them. Women get married.
Dull, dull. (see below)

IX

Jeannine came around to her brother's house the
next morning, just for fun. She had set her hair and
was wearing a swanky scarf over the curlers. Both Mrs.
Dadier and Jeannine know that there's nothing in a
breakfast nook to make it intrinsically interesting for
thirty years; nonetheless Jeannine giggles and twirls the
drinking straw in her breakfast cocoa fancifully this
way and that. It's the kind of straw that has a pleated
section in the middle like the bellows of a concertina.

"I always liked these when I was a little girl,"
Jeannine says.

"Oh my yes, didn't you," says Mrs. Dadier, who is
sitting with her second cup of coffee before attacking
the dishes.

Jeannine gives way to a fit of hysterics.

"Do you remember——?" she cries. "And do you
remember——!"

"Heavens, yes," says Mrs. Dadier. "Don't I,
though."

They sit, saying nothing.

"Did Frank call?" This is Mrs. Dadier, carefully

126

keeping her voice neutral because she knows how Jeannine hates interference in her own affairs. Jeannine makes a face and then laughs again. "Oh, give him time, Mother," she says. "It's only ten o'clock." She seems to see the funny side of it more than Mrs. Dadier does. "Bro," says the latter, "was up at five and Eileen and I got up at eight. I know this is your vacation, Jeannine, but in the country—"

"I *did* get up at eight," says Jeannine, aggrieved. (She's lying.) "I did. I walked around the lake. I don't know why you keep telling me how late I get up; that may have been true a long time ago but it's certainly not true now, and I resent your saying so." The sun has gone in again. When Bud isn't around, there's Jeannie to watch out for; Mrs. Dadier tries to anticipate her wishes and not disturb her.

"Well, I keep forgetting," says Mrs. Dadier. "Your silly old mother! Bud says I wouldn't remember my head if it wasn't screwed on." It doesn't work. Jeannine, slightly sulky, attacks her toast and jam, cramming a piece into her mouth cater-cornered. Jam drops on the table. Jeannine, implacably convicted of getting up late, is taking it out on the table-cloth. Getting up late is wallowing in sin. It's unforgivable. It's improper. Mrs. Dadier, with the misplaced courage of the doomed, chooses to ignore the jam stains and get on with the really important question, *viz.,* is Jeannine going to have a kitchenette of her own (although it will really belong to someone else, won't it) and is she going to be made to get up early, *i.e.,* Get Married. Mrs. Dadier says very carefully and placatingly:

"Darling, have you ever had any thoughts about—" but this morning, instead of flinging off in a rage, her daughter kisses her on the top of the head and announces, "I'm going to do the dishes."

"Oh, no," says Mrs. Dadier deprecatingly; "My goodness, don't. I don't mind." Jeannine winks at her. She feels virtuous (because of the dishes) and daring (because of something else). "Going to make a phone call," she says, sauntering into the living room. *Not doing the dishes.* She sits herself down in the rattan chair and twirls the pencil her mother always keeps by the telephone pad. She draws flowers on the pad and the profiles of girls whose eyes are nonetheless in full-face. Should she call X? Should she wait for X to call her? When he calls, should she be effusive or reserved? Comradely or distant? Should she tell X about Cal? If he asks her out for tonight, should she refuse? Where will she go if she does? She can't possibly call him, of course. But suppose she rings up Mrs. Dadier's friend with a message? *My mother asked me to tell you....* Jeannine's hand is actually on the telephone receiver when she notices that the hand is shaking: a sportswoman's eagerness for the chase. She laughs under her breath. She picks up the phone, trembling with eagerness, and dials X's number; it's happening at last. Everything is going well. Jeannine has almost in her hand the brass ring which will entitle her to everything worthwhile in life. It's only a question of time before X decides; surely she can keep him at arm's length until then, keep him fascinated; there's so much time you can take up with will-she-won't-she, so that hardly anything else has to be settled at all. She feels something for him, she really does. She wonders when the reality of it begins to hit you. Off in telephone never-never-land someone picks up the receiver, interrupting the last ring, footsteps approach and recede, someone is clearing their throat into the mouthpiece.

"Hello?" (It's his mother.) Jeannine glibly repeats the fake message she has practiced in her head; X's mother says, "Here's Frank. Frank, it's Jeannine Dadier." Horror. More footsteps.

"Hello?" says X.

"Oh my, it's you; I didn't know you were there," says Jeannine.

"Hey!" says X, pleased. This is even more than she has a right to expect, according to the rules.

"Oh, I just called to tell your mother something," says Jeannine, drawing irritable, jagged lines across her doodles on the telephone pad. She keeps trying to think of the night before, but all she can remember is Bud playing with his youngest daughter, the only time she's ever seen her brother get foolish. He bounces her on his knee and gets red in the face, swinging her about

128

his head while she screams with delight. "Silly Sally went to town! Silly Sally flew a-r-o-o-und!" Eileen usually rescues the baby on the grounds that she's getting too excited. For some reason this whole memory causes Jeannine great pain and she can hardly keep her mind on what she's saying.

"I thought you'd already gone," says Jeannine hastily. He's going on and on about something or other, the cost of renting boats on the lake or would she like to play tennis.

"Oh, I love tennis," says Jeannine, who doesn't even own a racket.

Would she like to come over that afternoon?

She leans away from the telephone to consult an imaginary appointment book, imaginary friends; she allows reluctantly that oh yes, she might have some free time. It would really be fun to brush up on her tennis. Not that she's really good, she adds hastily. X chuckles. Well, maybe. There are a few more commonplaces and she hangs up, bathed in perspiration and ready to weep. *What's the matter with me?* She should be happy, or at least smug, and here she is experiencing the keenest sorrow. What on earth for? She digs her pencil vindictively into the telephone pad as if it were somehow responsible. *Damn you.* Perversely, images of silly Cal come back to her, not nice ones, either. She has to pick up the phone again, after verifying an imaginary date with an imaginary acquaintance, and tell X yes or no; so Jeannine rearranges the scarf over her curlers, plays with a button on her blouse, stares miserably at her shoes, runs her hands over her knees, and makes up her mind. She's nervous. Masochistic. It's that old thing come back again about her not being good enough for good luck. That's nonsense and she knows it. She picks up the phone, smiling: tennis, drinks, dinner, back in the city a few more dates where he can tell her about school and then one night (hugging her a little extra hard)—"Jeannie, I'm getting my divorce." *My name is Jeannine.* The shopping will be fun. *I'm twenty-nine, after all.* It is with a sense of intense relief that she dials; the new life is beginning. She can do it, too. She's normal. She's as good as every

129

other girl. She starts to sing under her breath. The phone bell rings in Telephoneland and somebody comes to pick it up; she hears all the curious background noises of the relays, somebody speaking faintly very far away. She speaks quickly and distinctly, without the slightest hesitation now, remembering all those loveless nights with her knees poking up into the air, how she's discommoded and almost suffocated, how her leg muscles ache and she can't get her feet on the surface of the bed. Marriage will cure all that. The scrubbing uncleanably old linoleum and dusting the same awful things, week after week. But he's going places. She says boldly and decisively:

"Cal, come get me."

Shocked at her own treachery, she bursts into tears. She hears Cal say "Okay, baby," and he tells her what bus he'll be on.

"Cal!" she adds breathlessly; "You know that question you keep asking, sweetheart? Well, the answer is Yes." She hangs up, much eased. It'll be so much better once it's done. Foolish Jeannine, to expect anything else. It's an uncharted continent, marriage. She wipes her eyes with the back of her hand; X can go to hell. Making conversation is just work. She strolls into the kitchenette where she finds herself alone; Mrs. Dadier is outside in back, weeding a little patch of a garden all the Dadiers own in common; Jeannine takes the screen out of the kitchen window and leans out.

"Mother!" she says in a sudden flood of happiness and excitement, for the importance of what she has just done has suddenly become clear to her, "Mother!" (waving wildly out the window) "Guess what!" Mrs. Dadier, who is on her knees in the carrot bed, straightens up, shading her face with her one hand. "What is it, darling?"

"Mother, I'm getting married!" What comes after this will be very exciting, a sort of dramatic presentation, for Jeannine will have a big wedding. Mrs. Dadier drops her gardening trowel in sheer astonishment. She'll hurry inside, a tremendous elevation of mood enveloping both women; they will, in fact, embrace and kiss one another, and Jeannine will dance around the kitchen. "Wait 'til Bro hears about *this!*" Jeannine will exclaim. Both will cry. It's the first time in Jeannine's life that she's managed to do something perfectly O.K. And not too late, either. She thinks that perhaps the lateness of her marriage will be compensated for by a special mellowness; there must be, after all, some reason for all that experimenting, all that reluctance. She imagines the day she will be able to announce even better news: "Mother, I'm going to have a baby." Cal himself hardly figures in this at all, for Jeannine has forgotten his laconism, his passivity, his strange mournfulness unconnected to any clear emotion, his abruptness, how hard it is to get him to talk about anything. She hugs herself, breathless with joy, waiting for Mrs. Dadier to hurry inside; "My little baby!" Mrs. Dadier will say emotionally, embracing Jeannine. It seems to Jeannine that she has never known anything so solid and beautiful as the kitchen in the morning sunlight, with the walls glowing and everything so delicately outlined in light, so fresh and real. Jeannine, who has almost been killed by an unremitting and drastic discipline not of her own choosing, who has been maimed almost to death by a vigilant self-suppression quite irrelevant to anything she once wanted or loved, here finds her reward. This proves it is all right. Everything is indubitably good and indubitably real. She loves herself, and if I stand like Atropos in the corner, with my arm around the shadow of her dead self, if the other Jeannine (who is desperately tired and knows there is no freedom for her this side the grave) attempts to touch her as she whirls joyfully past, Jeannine does not see or hear it. At one stroke she has amputated her past. She's going to be fulfilled. She hugs herself and waits. That's all you have to do if you are a real, first-class Sleeping Beauty. She knows.

I'm so happy.

And there, but for the grace of God, go I.

PART SEVEN

I

I'll tell you how I turned into a man.

First I had to turn into a woman.

For a long time I had been neuter, not a woman at all but One Of The Boys, because if you walk into a gathering of men, professionally or otherwise, you might as well be wearing a sandwich board that says: LOOK! I HAVE TITS! there is this giggling and this chuckling and this reddening and this Uriah Heep twisting and writhing and this fiddling with ties and fixing of buttons and making of allusions and quoting of courtesies and this self-conscious gallantry plus a smirky insistence on my physique—all this dreary junk just to please me. If you get good at being One Of The Boys it goes away. Of course there's a certain disembodiment involved, but the sandwich board goes; I back-slapped and laughed at blue jokes, especially the hostile kind. Underneath you keep saying pleasantly but firmly No no no no no no. But it's necessary to my job and I like my job. I suppose they decided that my tits were not of the best kind, or not real, or that they were someone else's (my twin sister's), so they split me from the neck up; as I said, it demands a certain disembodiment. I thought that surely when I had acquired my Ph.D. and my professorship and my tennis medal and my engineer's contract and my ten thousand a year and my full-time housekeeper and my reputation and the respect of my colleagues, when I had grown strong, tall, and beautiful, when my I.Q. shot

133

past 200, when I had genius, *then* I could take off my sandwich board. I left my smiles and happy laughter at home. I'm not a woman; I'm a man. I'm a man with a woman's face. I'm a woman with a man's mind. Everybody says so. In my pride of intellect I entered a bookstore; I purchased a book; I no longer had to placate The Man; by God, I think I'm going to make it. I purchased a copy of John Stuart Mill's *The Subjection of Women;* now who can object to John Stuart Mill? He's dead. But the clerk did. With familiar archness he waggled his finger at me and said "tsk tsk"; all that writhing and fussing began again, what fun it was for him to have someone automatically not above reproach, and I knew beyond the shadow of a hope that to be female is to be mirror and honeypot, servant and judge, the terrible Rhadamanthus for whom he must perform but whose judgment is not human and whose services are at anyone's command, the vagina dentata and the stuffed teddy-bear he gets if he passes the test. This is until you're forty-five, ladies, after which you vanish into thin air like the smile of the Cheshire cat, leaving behind only a disgusting grossness and a subtle poison that automatically infects every man under twenty-one. Nothing can put you above this or below this or beyond it or outside of it, nothing, nothing, nothing at all, not your muscles or your brains, not being one of the boys or being one of the girls or writing books or writing letters or screaming or wringing your hands or cooking lettuce or being too tall or being too short or traveling or staying at home or ugliness or acne or diffidence or cowardice or perpetual shrinking and old age. In the latter cases you're only doubly damned. I went away—"forever feminine," as the man says—and I cried as I drove my car, and I wept by the side of the road (because I couldn't see and I might crash into something) and I howled and wrung my hands as people do only in medieval romances, for an American woman's closed car is the only place in which she can be alone (if she's unmarried) and the howl of a sick she-wolf carries around the world, whereupon the world thinks it's very comical. Privacy in cars and

134

bathrooms, what ideas we have! If they tell me about the pretty clothes again, I'll kill myself.

I had a five-year-old self who said: *Daddy won't love you.*

I had a ten-year-old self who said: *the boys won't play with you.*

I had a fifteen-year-old self who said: *nobody will marry you.*

I had a twenty-year-old self who said: *you can't be fulfilled without a child.* (A year there where I had recurrent nightmares about abdominal cancer which nobody would take out.)

I'm a sick woman, a madwoman, a ball-breaker, a man-eater; I don't consume men gracefully with my fire-like red hair or my poisoned kiss; I crack their joints with these filthy ghoul's claws and standing on one foot like a de-clawed cat, rake at your feeble efforts to save yourselves with my taloned hinder feet: my matted hair, my filthy skin, my big flat plaques of green bloody teeth. I don't think my body would sell anything. I don't think I would be good to look at. O of all diseases self-hate is the worst and I don't mean for the one who suffers it!

Do you know, all this time you preached at me? You told me that even Grendel's mother was actuated by maternal love.

You told me ghouls were male.

Rodan is male—and asinine.

King Kong is male.

I could have been a witch, but the Devil is male.

Faust is male.

The man who dropped the bomb on Hiroshima was male.

I was never on the moon.

Then there are the birds, with (as Shaw so nobly puts it) the touching poetry of their loves and nestings in which the males sing so well and beautifully and the females sit on the nest, and the baboons who get torn in half (female) by the others (male), and the chimpanzees with their hierarchy (male) written about by professors (male) with *their* hierarchy, who accept (male) the (male) view of (female) (male). You can see what's

135

happening. At heart I must be gentle, for I never even thought of the praying mantis or the female wasp; but I guess I am just loyal to my own phylum. One might as well dream of being an oak tree. Chestnut tree, great-rooted hermaphrodite. I won't tell you what poets and prophets my mind is crammed full of (Deborah, who said "Me, too, pretty please?" and got struck with leprosy), or Whom I prayed to (exciting my own violent hilarity) or whom I avoided on the street (male) or whom I watched on television (male) excepting in my hatred only—if I remember—Buster Crabbe, who is the former Flash Gordon and a swimming instructor (I think) in real life, and in whose humanly handsome, gentle, puzzled old face I had the absurd but moving fancy that I saw some reflection of my own bewilderment at our mutual prison. Of course I don't know him and no one is responsible for his shadow on the screen or what madwomen may see there; I lay in my bed (which is not male), made in a factory by a (male) designed by a (male) and sold to me by a (small male) with unusually bad manners. I mean unusually bad manners for anybody.

You see how *very different* this is from the way things used to be in the bad old days, say five years ago. New Yorkers (female) have had the right to abortion for almost a year now, if you can satisfy the hospital boards that you deserve bed-room and don't mind the nurses calling you Baby Killer; citizens of Toronto, Canada, have perfectly free access to contraception if they are willing to travel 100 miles to cross the border, I could smoke my very own cigarette if I smoked (and get my very own lung cancer). Forward, eternally forward! Some of my best friends are—I was about to say that some of my best friends are—my friends—

My friends are dead.

Whoever saw *women* scaring anybody? (This was while I thought it important to be able to scare people.) You cannot say, to paraphrase an old, good friend, that there are the plays of Shakespeare and Shakespeare was a woman, or that Columbus sailed the Atlantic and Columbus was a woman or that Alger Hiss was tried for treason and Alger Hiss was a woman. (Mata Hari

was not a spy; she was a fuckeress.) Anyway every-
boy (sorry) everybody knows that what women have
done that is really important is not to constitute a great,
cheap labor force that you can zip in when you're at
war and zip out again afterwards but to Be Mothers, to
form the coming generation, to give birth to them, to
nurse them, to mop floors for them, to love them, cook
for them, clean for them, change their diapers, pick up
after them, and mainly sacrifice themselves for them.
This is the most important job in the world. That's why
they don't pay you for it.

I cried, and then stopped crying because otherwise
I would never have stopped crying. Things come to an
awful dead center that way. You will notice that even
my diction is becoming feminine, thus revealing my
true nature; I am not saying "Damn" any more,
or "Blast"; I am putting in lots of qualifiers like
"rather," I am writing in these breathless little feminine
tags, she threw herself down on the bed, I have no
structure (she thought), my thoughts seep out shape-
lessly like menstrual fluid, it is all very female and
deep and full of essences, it is very primitive and full of
"and's," it is called "run-on sentences."

Very swampy in my mind. Very rotten and badly
off. I am a woman. I am a woman with a woman's
brain. I am a woman with a woman's sickness. I am a
woman with the wraps off, bald as an adder, God help
me and you.

II

Then I turned into a man.
This was slower and less dramatic.
I think it had something to do with the knowledge
you suffer when you're an outsider—I mean *suffer;* I
do not mean *undergo* or *employ* or *tolerate* or *use* or
enjoy or *catalogue* or *file away* or *entertain* or *possess*
or *have*.

That knowledge is, of course, the perception of all

experience through two sets of eyes, two systems of value, two habits of expectation, almost two minds. This is supposed to be an infallible recipe for driving you gaga. Chasing the hare Reconciliation with the hounds of Persistence—but there, you see? I'm not Sir Thomas Nasshe (or Lady Nasshe, either, tho' she never wrote a line, poor thing). Rightaway you start something, down comes the portcullis. Blap. To return to knowledge, I think it was seeing the lords of the earth at lunch in the company cafeteria that finally did me in; as another friend of mine once said, men's suits are designed to inspire confidence even if the men can't. But their *shoes*—! Dear God. And their *ears!* Jesus. The innocence, the fresh-faced naiveté of power. The childlike simplicity with which they trust their lives to the Black men who cook for them and their self-esteem and their vanity and their little dangles to me, who everything for them. Their ignorance, their utter, happy ignorance. There was the virgin We sacrificed on the company quad when the moon was full. (You thought a virgin meant a girl, didn't you?) There was Our thinking about housework—dear God, scholarly papers about housework, what could be more absurd! And Our parties where we pinched and chased Each Other. Our comparing the prices of women's dresses and men's suits. Our push-ups. Our crying in Each Other's company. Our gossip. Our trivia. All trivia, not worth an instant's notice by any rational being. If you see Us skulking through the bushes at the rising of the moon, don't look. And don't wait around. Watch the wall, my darling, you'd better. Like all motion, I couldn't feel it while it went on, but this is what you have to do:

To resolve contrarieties, unite them in your own person.

This means: in all hopelessness, in terror of your life, without a future, in the sink of the worst despair that you can endure and will yet leave you the sanity to make a choice—take in your bare right hand one naked, severed end of a high-tension wire. Take the other in your left hand. Stand in a puddle. (Don't worry about letting go; you can't.) Electricity favors the prepared mind, and if you interfere in this avalanche

138

by accident you will be knocked down dead, you will be charred like a cutlet, and your eyes will be turned to burst red jellies, but if those wires are your own wires—hang on. God will keep your eyes in your head and your joints knit one to the other. When She sends the high voltage alone, well, we've all experienced those little shocks—you just shed it over your outside like a duck and it does nothing to you—but when She roars down in high voltage and high amperage both, She is after your marrow-bones; you are making yourself a conduit for holy terror and the ecstasy of Hell. But only in that way can the wires heal themselves. Only in that way can they heal you. Women are not used to power; that avalanche of ghastly strain will lock your muscles and your teeth in the attitude of an electro-cuted rabbit, but you are a strong woman, you are God's favorite, and you can endure; if you can say "yes, okay, go on"—after all, where else can you go? What else can you do?—if you let yourself through yourself and into yourself and out of yourself, turn yourself inside out, give yourself the kiss of reconcilia-tion, marry yourself, love yourself—

Well, I turned into a man.

We love, says Plato, that in which we are defec-tive; when we see our magical Self in the mirror of an-other, we pursue it with desperate cries—*Stop! I must possess you!*—but if it obligingly stops and turns, how on earth can one then possess it? Fucking, if you will forgive the pun, is an anti-climax. And you are as poor as before. For years I wandered in the desert, crying: *Why do you torment me so?* and *Why do you hate me so?* and *Why do you put me down so?* and *I will abase myself* and *I will please you* and *Why, oh why have you forsaken me?* This is very feminine. What I learned late in life, under my rain of lava, under my kill-or-cure, unhappily, slowly, stubbornly, barely, and in really dreadful pain, was that there is one and only one way to possess that in which we are defective, therefore that which we need, therefore that which we want.

Become it.

(Man, one assumes, is the proper study of Man-kind. Years ago we were all cave Men. Then there is

Java Man and the future of Man and the values of Western Man and existential Man and economic Man and Freudian Man and the Man in the moon and modern Man and eighteenth-century Man and too many Mans to count or look at or believe. There is Mankind. An eerie twinge of laughter garlands these paradoxes. For years I have been saying *Let me in, Love me, Approve me, Define me, Regulate me, Validate me, Support me.* Now I say *Move over.* If we are all Mankind, it follows to my interested and righteous and rightnow very bright and beady little eyes, that I too am a Man and not at all a Woman, for honestly now, whoever heard of Java Woman and existential Woman and the values of Western Woman and scientific Woman and alienated nineteenth-century Woman and all the rest of that dingy and antiquated rag-bag? All the rags in it are White, anyway. I think I am a Man; I think you had better call me a Man; I think you will write about me as a Man from now on and speak of me as a Man and employ me as a Man and recognize child-rearing as a Man's business; you will think of me as a Man and treat me as a Man until it enters your muddled, terrified, preposterous, nine-tenths-fake, loveless, papier-mâché-bull-moose head that *I am a man.* (And you are a woman.) That's the whole secret. Stop hugging Moses' tablets to your chest, nitwit; you'll cave in. Give me your Linus blanket, child. Listen to the female man.

If you don't, by God and all the Saints, *I'll break your neck.*)

III

We would gladly have listened to her (they said) *if only she had spoken like a lady.* But they are liars and the truth is not in them.

Shrill ... vituperative ... no concern for the future of society ... maunderings of antiquated feminism ... selfish femlib ... needs a good lay ... this shapeless book . . . of course a calm and objective discussion is beyond . . . twisted, neurotic . . . some truth buried in a largely hysterical . . . of very limited interest, I should . . . another tract for the trash-can . . . burned her bra and thought that . . . no characterization, no plot . . . really important issues are neglected while . . . hermetically sealed . . . women's limited experience . . . another of the screaming sisterhood . . . a not very appealing aggressiveness . . . could have been done with wit if the author had . . . deflowering the pretentious male . . . a man would have given his right arm to . . . hardly girlish . . . a woman's book . . . another shrill polemic which the . . . a mere male like myself can hardly . . . a brilliant but basically confused study of feminine hysteria which . . . feminine lack of objectivity . . . this pretense at a novel . . . trying to shock . . . the tired tricks of the anti-novelists . . . how often must a poor critic have to . . . the usual boring obligatory references to Lesbianism . . . denial of the profound sexual polarity which . . . an all too womanly refusal to face facts . . . pseudo-masculine brusqueness . . . the ladies'-magazine level . . . trivial topics like housework and the predictable screams of . . . those who cuddled up to ball-breaker Kate will . . . unfortunately sexless in its outlook . . . drivel . . . a warped clinical protest against . . . violently waspish attack . . . formidable self-pity which erodes any chance of . . . formless . . . the inability to accept the female role which . . . the predictable fury at anatomy displaced to . . . without the grace and compassion which we have the right to expect . . . anatomy is destiny . . . destiny is anatomy . . . sharp and funny but without real weight or anything beyond a topical . . . just plain bad . . . we "dear ladies," whom Russ would do away with, unfortunately just don't *feel* . . . ephemeral trash, missiles of the sex war . . . a female lack of experience which. . . .

Q.E.D. Quod erat demonstrandum. It has been proved.

IV

Janet has begun to follow strange men on the street; whatever will become of her? She does this either out of curiosity or just to annoy me; whenever she sees someone who interests her, woman or man, she swerves automatically (humming a little tune, da-dum, da-dee) and continues walking but in the opposite direction. When Whileawayan 1 meets Whileawayan 2, the first utters a compound Whileawayan word which may be translated as "Hello-yes?" to which the answer may be the same phrase repeated (but without the rising inflection), "Hello-no," "Hello" alone, silence, or "No!" "Hello-yes" means *I wish to strike up a conversation;* "Hello" means *I don't mind your remaining here but I don't wish to talk;* "Hello-no" *Stay here if you like but don't bother me in any way;* silence *I'd be much obliged if you'd get out of here; I'm in a foul temper.* Silence accompanied by a quick shake of the head means *I'm not ill-tempered but I have other reasons for wanting to be alone.* "No!" means *Get away or I'll do that to you which you won't like.* (In contradistinction to our customs, it is the late-comer who has the moral edge, Whileawayan 1 having already got some relief or enjoyment out of the convenient bench or flowers or spectacular mountain or whatever's at issue.) Each of these responses may be used as salutations, of course.

I asked Janet what happens if both Whileawayans say "No!"

"Oh" she says (bored), "they fight."

"Usually one of us runs away," she added.

Janet is sitting next to Laura Rose on my nubbly-brown couch, half-asleep, half all over her friend in a confiding way, her head resting on Laur's responsible shoulder. A young she-tiger with a large, floppy cub. In her dozing Janet has shed ten years' anxiety and twenty pounds of trying-to-impress-others; she must be so much younger and sillier with her own people; grubbing in the tomato patch or chasing lost cows; what Safety and Peace officers do is beyond me. (A cow found her way into the Mountainpersons' common room and backed a stranger through a foam wall by trying to start a conversation—Whileawayans have a passion for improving the capacities of domestic animals—she kept nudging this visitor and saying "Friend? Friend?" in a great, wistful moo, like the monster in the movie, until a Mountainperson shooed her away: *You don't want to make trouble, do you, child? You want to be milked, don't you? Come on, now.*)

"Tell us about the cow," says Laura Rose. "Tell Jeannine about it," (who's vainly trying to flow into the wall, O agony, those two women are *touching*).

"No," mutters Janet sleepily.

"Then tell us about the Zdubakovs," says Laur.

"You're a vicious little beast!" says Janet and sits bolt upright.

"Oh come on, giraffe," says Laura Rose. "Tell!" She has sewn embroidered bunches of flowers all over her denim jacket and jeans with a red, red rose on the crotch, but she doesn't wear these clothes at home, only when visiting.

"You are a damned vicious cublet," said Janet. "I'll tell you something to sweeten your disposition. Do you want to hear about the three-legged goat who skipped off to the North Pole?"

"No," says Laur. Jeannine flattens like a film of oil; she vanishes dimly into a cupboard, putting her fingers in her ears.

"Tell!" says Laur, twisting my little finger. I bury my face in my hands. Ay, no. Ay, no. Laura must hear. She kissed my neck and then my ear in a passion for all the awful things I do as S & P; I straightened up and rocked back and forth. The trouble with you people is you get no charge from death. Myself, it shakes me all over. Somebody I'd never met had left a note saying the usual thing: *ha ha on you, you do not exist, go away,* for we are so bloody cooperative that we have this solipsistic underside, you see? So I went up-mountain and found her; I turned on my two-way vocal three hundred yards from criminal Elena Twason and said, "Well, well, Elena, you shouldn't take a vacation without notifying your friends."

"Vacation?" she says; "Friends? Don't lie to me, girl. You read my letter," and by this I began to understand that she hadn't had to go mad to do this and that was terrible. I said, "What letter? Nobody found a letter."

"The cow ate it," says Elena Twason. "Shoot me. I don't believe you're there but my body believes; I believe that my tissues believe in the bullet that you do not believe in yourself, and that will kill me."

"Cow?" says I, ignoring the rest, "what cow? You Zdubakovs don't keep cows. You're vegetable-and-goat people, I believe. Quit joking with me, Elena. Come back; you went botanizing and lost your way, that's all."

"Oh *little girl*," she said, so off-hand, so good-humored, *"little child,* don't deform reality. Don't mock us both." In spite of the insults, I tried again.

"What a pity," I said, "that your hearing is going so bad at the age of sixty, Elena Twa. Or perhaps it's my own. I thought I heard you say something else. But the echoes in this damned valley are enough to make anything unintelligible; I could have sworn that I was offering you an illegal collusion in an untruth and that like a sensible, sane woman, you were accepting." I could see her white hair through the binoculars; she could've been my mother. Sorry for the banality, but it's true. Often they try to kill you so I showed myself as best I could, but she didn't move—exhausted? Sick? Nothing happened.

"Elena!" I shouted. "By the entrails of God, will you please come down!" and I waved my arms like a semaphore. I thought: *I'll wait until morning at least. I can do that much.* In my mind we changed places several times, she and I, both of us acting as illegally in our respective positions as we could, but I might be able to patch up some sort of story. As I watched her, she began to amble down the hillside, that little white patch of hair bobbing through the autumn foliage like a deer's tail. Chuckling to herself, idly swinging a stick she'd picked up: weak little thing, just a twig really, too dry to hit anything without breaking. I ambled ghostly beside her; it's so pretty in the mountains at that time of year, everything burns and burns without heat. I think she was enjoying herself, having finally put herself, as it were, beyond the reach of consequences; she took her little stroll until we were quite close to each other, close enough to converse face to face, perhaps as far as I am from you. She had made herself a crown of scarlet maple leaves and put it on her head, a little askew because it was a little too big to fit. She smiled at me.

"Face facts," she said. Then, drawing down the corners of her mouth with an ineffable air of gaiety and arrogance:

"Kill, killer."

So I shot her.

Laur, who has been listening intently all this time, bloodthirsty little devil, takes Janet's face in her hands. "Oh, come on. You shot her with a narcotic, that's all. You told me so. A narcotic dart."

"No," said Janet. "I'm a liar. I killed her. We use explosive bullets because it's almost always distance work. I have a rifle like the kind you've often seen yourself."

"Aaaah!" is Laura Rose's long, disbelieving, angry comment. She came over to me: "Do *you* believe it?" (I shall have to drag Jeannine out of the woodwork with both hands.) Still angry, Laur straddles the room with her arms clasped behind her back. Janet is either asleep or acting. I wonder what Laur and Janet do in bed; what do women think of women?

"I don't care what either of you thinks of me," says Laur. "I like it! By God, I like the idea of doing something to somebody for a change instead of having it done to me. Why are you in Safety and Peace if you don't enjoy it!"

"I told you," says Janet softly.

Laur said, "I know, someone has to do it. Why you?"

"I was assigned."

145

"Why? Because you're bad! You're tough." (She smiles at her own extravagance. Janet sat up, wavering a little, and shook her head.)

"Dearest, I'm not good for much; understand that. Farm work or forest work, what else? I have some gift to unravel these human situations, but it's not quite intelligence."

"Which is why you're an emissary?" says Laur. "Don't expect me to believe that." Janet stares at my rug. She yawns, jaw-cracking. She clasps her hands loosely in her lap, remembering perhaps what it had been like to carry the body of a sixty-year-old woman down a mountainside: at first something you wept over, then something horrible, then something only distasteful, and finally you just did it.

"I am what you call an emissary," she said slowly, nodding courteously to Jeannine and me, "for the same reason that I was in S & P. I'm expendable, my dear. Laura, Whileawayan intelligence is confined in a narrower range than yours; we are not only smarter on the average but there is much less spread on either side of the average. This helps our living together. It also makes us extremely intolerant of routine work. But still there is some variation." She lay back on the couch, putting her arms under her head. Spoke to the ceiling. Dreaming, perhaps. Of Vittoria?

"Oh, honey," she said, "I'm here because they can do without me. I was S & P because they could do without me. There's only one reason for that, Laur, and it's very simple.

"I am stupid."

Janet sleeps or pretends to, Joanna knits (that's me), Jeannine is in the kitchen. Laura Rose, still resentfully twitching with unconquered Genghis Khanism, takes a book from my bookshelf and lies on her stomach on the rug. I believe she is reading an art book, something she isn't interested in. The house seems asleep. In the desert between the three of us the dead Elena Twason Zdubakov begins to take shape; I give her Janet's eyes, Janet's frame, but bent with age, some of Laur's impatient sturdiness but modified with the graceful trembling of old age: her papery skin, her

146

smile, the ropy muscles on her wasted arms, her white hair cut in an economical kind of thatch. Helen's belly is loose with old age, her face wrinkled, a never-attractive face like that of an extremely friendly and intelligent horse: long and droll. The lines about her mouth would be comic lines. She's wearing a silly kind of khaki shorts-and-shirt outfit which is not really what Whileawayans wear, but I give it to her anyway. Her ears are pierced. Her mountain twig has become a carved jade pipe covered with scenes of vines, scenes of people crossing bridges, people pounding flax, processions of cooks or grain-bearers. She wears a spray of red mountain-ash berries behind one ear. Elena is about to speak; from her comes a shock of personal strength, a wry impressiveness, an intelligence so powerful that in spite of myself I open my arms to this impossible body, this walking soul, this somebody's grandma who could say with such immense élan to her legal assassin, "Face facts, child." No man in our world would touch Elena. In Whileawayan leaf-red pajamas, in silver silk overalls, in the lengths of moony brocade in which Whileawayans wrap themselves for pleasure, this would be a beautiful Helen. Elena Twason swathed in cut-silk brocade, nipping a corner of it for fun. It would be delightful to have erotic play with Elena Twason; I feel this on my lips and tongue, in the palms of my hands, all my inside skin. I feel it down below, in my sex. What a formidable woman! Shall I laugh or cry? She's dead, though—killed dead—so never shall Ellie Twa's ancient legs entwine with mine or twiddle from under the shell of a computer housing, crossing and uncrossing her toes as she and the computer tell each other uproarious jokes. Her death was a bad joke. I would like very much to make love skin-to-skin with Elena Twason Zdubakov, but she is thank-the-male-God dead and Jeannine can come shudderingly out of the woodwork. Laur and Janet have gone to sleep together on the couch as if they were in a Whileawayan common bedroom, which is not for orgies, as you might think, but for people who are lonesome, for children, for people who have nightmares. We miss those innocent hairy sleepies we used to tangle with

147

back in the dawn of time before some progressive nit-wit took to deferred gratification and chipping flint.

"What's this?" whispered Jeannine, furtively proffering something for my inspection.

"I don't know, is it a staple gun?" I said. (It had a handle.) "Whose is it?"

"I found it on Janet's bed," said Jeannine, still whispering. "Just lying there. I think she took it out of her suitcase. I can't figure out what it is. You hold it by the handle and if you move this switch it buzzes on one end, though I don't see why, and another switch makes this piece move up and down. But that seems to be an attachment. It doesn't look as if it's been used as much as the rest of it. The handle's really something; it's all carved and decorated."

"Put it back," I said.

"But what *is* it?" said Jeannine.

"A Whileawayan communications device," I said. "Put it back, Jeannie."

"Oh?" she said. Then she looked doubtfully at me and at the sleepers. Janet, Jeannine, Joanna. Something very J-ish is going on here.

"Is it dangerous?" said Jeannine. I nodded—emphatically.

"Infinitely," I said. "It can blow you up."

"All of me?" said Jeannine, holding the thing gingerly at arm's length.

"What it does to your body," said I, choosing my words with extreme care, "is nothing compared to what it does to your mind, Jeannine. It will ruin your mind. It will explode in your brains and drive you crazy. You will never be the same again. You will be lost to respectability and decency and decorum and dependency and all sorts of other nice, normal things beginning with a D. It will kill you, Jeannine. You will be dead, dead, dead.

"Put it back."

(On Whileaway these charming dinguses are heirlooms. They are menarchal gifts, presented after all sorts of glass-blowing, clay-modeling, picture-painting, ring-dancing, and Heaven knows what sort of silliness done by the celebrants to honor the little girl whose celebration it is. There is a tremendous amount of kissing and hand-shaking. This is only the formal presentation, of course; cheap, style-less models that you wouldn't want to give as presents are available to everybody long before this. Whileawayans often become quite fond of them, as you or I would of a hi-fi set or a sports car, but all the same, a machine's only a machine. Janet later offered to lend me hers on the grounds that she and Laur no longer needed it.)

Jeannine stood there with an expression of extraordinary distrust: Eve and the hereditary instinct that tells her to beware of apples. I took her by the shoulders, telling her again that it was a radar set. That it was extremely dangerous. That it would blow up if she wasn't careful. Then I pushed her out of the room.

"Put it back."

V

Jeannine, Janet, Joanna. Something's going to happen. I came downstairs in my bathrobe at three A.M., unable to sleep. This house ought to be ringed with government spies, keeping their eyes on our diplomat from the stars and her infernal, perverted friends, but nobody's about. I met Jeannine in the kitchen in her pajamas, looking for the cocoa. Janet, still in sweater and slacks, was reading at the kitchen table, puffy-eyed from lack of sleep. She was cross-noting Gunnar Myrdal's *An American Dilemma and 'Marital Patterns of Nebraska College Sophomores, 1938–1948.*

Jeannine said:

"I try to make the right decisions, but things don't work out. I don't know why. Other women are so happy. I was a very good student when I was a little girl and I liked school tremendously, but then when I got to be around twelve, everything changed. Other things become important then, you know. It's not that I'm not attractive; I'm pretty enough, I mean in a usual way, goodness knows I'm no beauty. But that's all

149

right. I love books, I love reading and thinking, but Cal says it's only daydreaming; I just don't know. What do you think? There's my cat, Mister Frosty, you've seen him, I'm terribly fond of him, as much as you can be of an animal, I suppose, but can you make a life out of books and a cat? I want to get married. It's there, you know, somewhere just around the corner; sometimes after coming out of the ballet or the theatre, I can almost feel it, I know if only I could turn around in the right direction, I'd be able to reach out my hand and take it. Things will get better. I suppose I'm just late in developing. Do you think if I got married I would like making love better? Do you think there's unconscious guilt—you know, because Cal and I aren't married? I don't feel it that way, but if it was unconscious, you wouldn't feel it, would you? Sometimes I get really blue, really awful, thinking: suppose I get old this way? Suppose I reach fifty or sixty and it's all been the same—that's horrible—but of course it's impossible. It's ridiculous. I ought to get busy at something. Cal says I'm frightfully lazy. We're getting married— marvelous!—and my mother's very pleased because I'm twenty-nine. Under the wire, you know, oops! Sometimes I think I'll get a notebook and write down my dreams because they're very elaborate and interesting, but I haven't yet. Maybe I won't; it's a silly thing to do. Do you think so? My sister-in-law's so happy and Bud's happy and I know my mother is; and Cal has a great future planned out. And if I were a cat I would be my cat, Mister Frosty, and I'd be spoiled rotten (Cal says). I have everything and yet I'm not happy.

"Sometimes I want to die."

Then Joanna said:

"After we had finished making love, he turned to the wall and said, 'Woman, you're lovely. You're sensuous. You should wear long hair and lots of eye make-up and tight clothing.' Now what does this have to do with anything? I remain bewildered. I have a devil of pride and a devil of despair; I used to go out among the hills at seventeen (this is a poetic euphemism for a suburban golf course) and there, on my knees, I swear it, knelen on my kne, I wept aloud, I

150

wrung my hands, crying: I am a poet! I am Shelley! I am a genius! What has any of this to do with me! The utter irrelevancy. The inanity of the whole business. Lady, your slip's showing. God bless. At eleven I passed an eighth-grader, a boy, who muttered between his teeth, 'Shake it but don't break it.' The career of the sexless sex object had begun. I had, at seventeen, an awful conversation with my mother and father in which they told me how fine it was to be a girl—the pretty clothes (why are people so obsessed with this?) and how I did not have to climb Everest, but could listen to the radio and eat bon-bons while my Prince was out doing it. When I was five my indulgent Daddy told me he made the sun come up in the morning and I expressed my skepticism; 'Well, watch for it tomorrow and you'll see,' he said. I learned to watch his face for cues as to what I should do or what I should say, or even what I should see. For fifteen years I fell in love with a different man every spring like a berserk cuckoo-clock. I love my body dearly and yet I would copulate with a rhinoceros if I could become not-a-woman. There is the vanity training, the obedience training, the self-effacement training, the deference training, the dependency training, the passivity training, the rivalry training, the stupidity training, the placation training. How am I to put this together with my human life, my intellectual life, my solitude, my transcendence, my brains, and my fearful, fearful ambition? I failed miserably and thought it was my own fault. You can't unite woman and human any more than you can unite matter and anti-matter; they are designed not to be stable together and they make just as big an explosion inside the head of the unfortunate girl who believes in both.

"Do you enjoy playing with other people's children—for ten minutes? Good! This reveals that you have Maternal Instinct and you will be forever wretched if you do not instantly have a baby of your own (or three or four) and take care of that unfortunate victimized object twenty-four hours a day, seven days a week, fifty-two weeks a year, for eighteen years, all by yourself. (Don't expect much help.)

"Are you lonely? Good! This shows that you have Feminine Incompleteness; get married and do all your husband's personal services, buck him up when he's low, teach him about sex (if he wants you to), praise his technique (if he doesn't), have a family if he wants a family, follow him if he changes cities, get a job if he needs you to get a job, and this too goes on seven days a week, fifty-two weeks a year forever and ever amen unless you find yourself a divorcée at thirty with (probably two) small children. (Be a shrew and ruin yourself, too, how about it?)

"Do you like men's bodies? Good! This is beginning to be almost as good as getting married. This means that you have True Womanliness, which is fine unless you want to do it with him on the bottom and you on the top, or any other way than he wants to do it, or you don't come in two minutes, or you don't want to do it, or you change your mind in mid-course, or get aggressive, or show your brains, or resent never being talked to, or ask him to take you out, or fail to praise him, or worry about whether he Respects You, or hear yourself described as a whore, or develop affectionate feelings for him (see Feminine Incompleteness, above) or resent the predation you have to face and screen out so unremittingly—

"I am a telephone pole, a Martian, a rose-bed, a tree, a floor lamp, a camera, a scarecrow. I'm not a woman.

"Well, it's nobody's fault, I know (this is what I'm supposed to think). I know and totally approve and genuflect to and admire and wholly obey the doctrine of Nobody's Fault, the doctrine of Gradual Change, the doctrine that Women Can Love Better Than Men so we ought to be saints (warrior saints?), the doctrine of It's A Personal Problem.

"(Selah, selah, there is only one True Prophet and it's You, don't kill me, massa, I'se jes' ig'nerant.)

"You see before you a woman in a trap. Those spike-heeled shoes that blow your heels off (so you become round-heeled). The intense need to smile at everybody. The slavish (but respectable) adoration: Love me or I'll die. As the nine-year-old daughter of my friend painstakingly carved on her linoleum block when the third grade was doing creative printing: I am like I am suppose to be Otherwise I'd kill myself Rachel.

"Would you believe—could you hear without laughing—could you credit without positively oofing your sides with hysterical mirth, that for years my secret, teenage ambition—more important than washing my hair even and I wouldn't tell it to *anybody*—was to stand up fearless and honest like Joan of Arc or Galileo—

"And suffer for the truth?"

So Janet said:

"Life has to end. What a pity! Sometimes, when one is alone, the universe presses itself into one's hands: a plethora of joy, an organized plenitude. The iridescent, peacock-green folds of the mountains in South Continent, the cobalt-colored sky, the white sunlight which makes everything too real to be true. The existence of existence always amazes me. You tell me that men are supposed to like challenge, that it is risk that makes them truly men, but if I—a foreigner—may venture an opinion, what we know beyond any doubt is that the world is a bath; we bathe in air, as Saint Teresa said the fish is in the sea and the sea is in the fish. I fancy your old church windows wished to show worshippers' faces stained with that emblematic brightness. Do you really want to take risks? Inoculate yourself with bubonic plague. What foolishness! When that intellectual sun rises, the pure sward lengthens under the crystal mountain; under that pure intellectual light there is neither material pigment nor no true shadow any more, any more. What price ego then?

"Now you tell me that enchanted frogs turn into princes, that frogesses under a spell turn into princesses. What of it? Romance is bad for the mind. I'll tell you a story about the old Whileawayan philosopher—she is a folk character among us, rather funny in an odd way, or as we say, 'ticklish.' The Old Whileawayan Philosopher was sitting cross-legged among her disciples (as usual) when, without the slightest explana-

153

tion, she put her fingers into her vagina, withdrew them, and asked, 'What have I here?'

"The disciples all thought very deeply.

" 'Life,' said one young woman.

" 'Power,' said another.

" 'Housework,' said a third.

" 'The passing of time,' said the fourth, 'and the tragic irreversibility of organic truth.'

"The Old Whileawayan Philosopher hooted. She was immensely entertained by this passion for myth-making. 'Exercise your projective imaginations,' she said, 'on people who can't fight back,' and opening her hand, she showed them that her fingers were perfectly unstained by any blood whatever, partly because she was one hundred and three years old and long past the menopause and partly because she had just died that morning. She then thumped her disciples severely about the head and shoulders with her crutch and vanished. Instantly two of the disciples achieved Enlightenment, the third became violently angry at the imposture and went to live as a hermit in the mountains, while the fourth—entirely disillusioned with philosophy, which she concluded to be a game for crackpots—left philosophizing forever to undertake the dredging out of silted-up harbors. What became of the Old Philosopher's ghost is not known. Now the moral of this story is that all images, ideals, pictures, and fanciful representations tend to vanish sooner or later unless they have the great good luck to be exuded from within, like bodily secretions or the bloom on a grape. And if you think that grape-bloom is romantically pretty, you ought to know that it is in reality a film of yeasty parasites rioting on the fruit and gobbling up grape sugar, just as the human skin (under magnification, I admit) shows itself to be iridescent with hordes of plantlets and swarms of beasties and all the scum left by their dead bodies. And according to our Whileawayan notions of propriety all this is just as it should be and an occasion for infinite rejoicing.

"After all, why slander frogs? Princes and princesses are fools. They do nothing interesting in your stories. They are not even real. According to history books you passed through the stage of feudal social organization in Europe some time ago. Frogs, on the other hand, are covered with mucus, which they find delightful; they suffer agonies of passionate desire in which the males will embrace a stick or your finger if they cannot get anything better, and they experience rapturous, metaphysical joy (of a froggy sort, to be sure) which shows plainly in their beautiful, chrysoberyllian eyes.

"How many princes or princesses can say as much?"

Joanna, Jeannine, and Janet. What a feast of J's. Somebody is collecting J's.

We were somewhere else. I mean we were not in the kitchen any more. Janet was still wearing her slacks and sweater, I my bathrobe, and Jeannine her pajamas. Jeannine was carrying a half-empty cup of cocoa with a spoon stuck in it.

But we were somewhere else.

PART EIGHT

I

Who am I?

I know who I am, but what's my brand name?

Me with a new face, a puffy mask. Laid over the old one in strips of plastic that hurt when they come off, a blond Hallowe'en ghoul on top of the S.S. uniform. I was skinny as a beanpole underneath except for the hands, which were similarly treated, and that very impressive face. I did this once in my line of business, which I'll go into a little later, and scared the idealistic children who lived downstairs. Their delicate skins red with offended horror. Their clear young voices raised in song (at three in the morning).

I don't do this often (say I, the ghoul) but it's great elevator technique, sticking your forefinger to the back of somebody's neck while passing the fourth floor, knowing that he'll never find out that you haven't a gun and that you're not all there.

(Sorry. But watch out.)

II

Whom did we meet in that matron blackness but The Woman Who Has No Brand Name.

"I suppose you are wondering," she said (and I enjoyed her enjoyment of my enjoyment of her enjoyment of that cliché) "why I have brought you here."

157

We did.

We wondered why we were in a white-walled penthouse living room overlooking the East River at night with furniture so sharp-edged and ultra-modern that you could cut yourself on it, with a wall-length bar, with a second wall hung entirely in black velvet like a stage, with a third wall all glass, outside which the city did not look quite as I remembered it.

Now J (as I shall call her) is really terrifying, for she's invisible. Against the black curtains her head and hands float in sinister disconnection, like puppets controlled by separate strings. There are baby spotlights in the ceiling, which illuminate in deep chiaroscuro her gray hair, her lined face, her rather macabre grin, for her teeth seem to be one fused ribbon of steel. She stepped out against the white wall, a woman-shaped hole, a black cardboard cut-out; with a crooked, charming smile she clapped her hand to her mouth, either taking something out or putting something in—see? Real teeth. Those disbodied, almost crippled hands clasped themselves. She sat on her black leather couch and vanished again; she smiled and dropped fifteen years; she has silver hair, not gray, and I don't know how old she is. How she loves us! She leans forward and croons at us like Garbo. Jeannine has sunk down into a collection of glass plates that passes for a chair; her cup and spoon make a tiny, spineless chattering. Janet is erect and ready for anything.

"I'm glad, so glad, so very glad," says J softly. She doesn't mind Jeannine's being a coward. She turns the warmth of her smile on Jeannine the way none of us has ever been smiled at before, a dwelling, loving look that would make Jeannine go through fire and water to get it again, the kind of mother-love whose lack gets into your very bones.

"I am called Alice Reasoner," says J, "christened Alice-Jael; I am an employee of the Bureau of Comparative Ethnology. My code name is Sweet Alice; can you believe it?" (with a soft, cultivated laugh) "Look around you and welcome yourselves; look at me and make me welcome; welcome myself, welcome me, welcome I," and leaning forward, a shape stamped by a cookie-cutter on to nothing, with pleasant art and sincere gestures, Alice-Jael Reasoner told us what you have no doubt guessed long, long ago.

III

(Her real laugh is the worst human sound I have ever heard: a hard, screeching yell that ends in gasps and rusty sobbing, as if some mechanical vulture on a gigantic garbage heap on the surface of the moon were giving one forced shriek for the death of all organic life. Yet J likes it. This is her *private* laugh. Alice is crippled, too; the ends of her fingers (she says) were once caught in a press and are growing cancerous—and to be sure, if you look at them closely you can see folds of loose, dead skin over the ends of her fingernails. She has hairpin-shaped scars under her ears, too.

IV

(Her pointed fingernails painted silver to distract the eye, Alice-Jael plays with the window console: the East River clouds over to reveal (serially) a desert morning, a black lava beach, and the surface of the moon. She sat, watching the pictures change, tapping her silver nails on the couch, herself the very picture of boredom. Come up close and you'll see that her eyes are silver, most unnatural. It came to me that we had been watching this woman perform for half an hour and had given not one thought to what might be happening around us or to us or behind us. The East River?

("An artist's conception," she says.)

V

"I am," says Jael Reasoner, "an employee of the Bureau of Comparative Ethnology and a specialist in disguises. It came to me several months ago that I might find my other selves out there in the great, gray might-have-been, so I undertook—for reasons partly personal and partly political, of which more later—to get hold of the three of you. It was very hard work. I'm a field worker and not a theoretician, but you must know that the closer to home you travel, the more power it takes, both to discriminate between small degrees of difference and to transport objects from one universe of probability into another.

"If we admit among the universes of probability any in which the laws of physical reality are different from our own, we will have an infinite number of universes. If we restrict ourselves to the laws of physical reality as we know them, we will have a limited number. Our universe is quantized; therefore the differences between possible universes (although very small) must be similarly quantized, and the number of such universes must be finite (although very large). I take it that it must be possible to distinguish the very smallest differences—say, that of one quantum of light—for otherwise we could not find our way to the same universe time after time, nor could we return to our own. Current theory has it that one cannot return to one's own past, but only to other people's; similarly one cannot travel into one's own future, but only to other people's, and in no way can these motions be forced to result in straightforward travel—*from any baseline whatever*. The only possible motion is diagonal motion. So you see that the classical paradoxes of time-travel simply do not apply—we cannot kill our own grandmothers and thereby cease to exist, nor can we travel into our own future and affect it in advance, so to speak. Nor can I, once I have made contact with your present, travel into your past or your future. The best I can do in finding out my own future is to study one very close to my own, but here the cost of power becomes prohibitive. My Department's researches are therefore conducted in regions rather far from home. Go too far and you find an Earth too close to the sun or too far away or nonexistent or barren of life; come too close and it costs too much. We operate in a pretty small optimal range. And of course I was doing this on my own, which means I must steal the whole damn operation anyway.

"You, Janet, were almost impossible to find. The universe in which your Earth exists does not even register on our instruments; neither do those for quite a probable spread on either side of you; we have been trying for years to find out why. Besides you are too close to us to be economically feasible. I had located Jeannine and not Joanna; you very obligingly stepped out of place and became as visible as a sore thumb; I've had a fix on you ever since. The three of you got together and I pulled you all in. Look at yourselves.

"Genetic patterns sometimes repeat themselves from possible present universe to possible present universe; this is also one of the elements that can vary between universes. There is repetition of genotypes in the far future too, sometimes. Here is Janet from the far future, but not my future or yours; here are the two of you from almost the same moment of time (but not as you see it!), both of those moments only a little behind mine; yet I won't happen in the world of either of you. We are less alike than identical twins, to be sure, but much more alike than strangers have any right to be. Look at yourselves again.

"We're all white-skinned, eh? I bet two of you didn't think of that. We're all women. We are tall, within a few inches of each other. Given a reasonable variation, we are the same racial type, even the same physical type—no redheads or olive skins, hm? Don't go by me; I'm not natural! Look in each other's faces. What you see is essentially the same genotype, modified by age, by circumstances, by education, by diet, by learning, by God knows what. Here is Jeannine, the youngest of us all with her smooth face: tall, thin,

161

sedentary, round-shouldered, a long-limbed body made of clay and putty; she's always tired and probably has trouble waking up in the morning. Hm? And there's Joanna, somewhat older, much more active, with a different gait, different mannerisms, quick and jerky, not depressed, sits with her spine like a ruler. Who'd think it was the same woman? There's Janet, hardier than the two of you put together, with her sun-bleached hair and her muscles; she's spent her life outdoors, a Swedish hiker and a farmhand. You begin to see? She's older and that masks a good deal. And of course she has had all the Whileawayan improvements—no rheumatism, no sinus trouble, no allergies, no appendix, good feet, good teeth, no double joints, and so forth and so forth, all the rest that we three must suffer. And I, who could throw you all across the room, though I don't look it. Yet we started the same. It's possible that in biological terms Jeannine is potentially the most intelligent of us all; try to prove that to a stranger! We ought to be equally long-lived but we won't be. We ought to be equally healthy but we're not. If you discount the wombs that bore us, our pre-natal nourishment, and our deliveries (none of which differ essentially) we ought to have started out with the same autonomic nervous system, the same adrenals, the same hair and teeth and eyes, the same circulatory system, and the same innocence. We ought to think alike and feel alike and act alike, but of course we don't. So plastic is humankind! Do you remember the old story of the Doppelgänger? This is the double you recognize instantly, with whom you feel a mysterious kinship. An instant sympathy, that informs you at once that the other is really your very own self. The truth is that people don't recognize themselves except in mirrors, and sometimes not even then. Between our dress, and our opinions, and our habits, and our beliefs, and our values, and our mannerisms, and our manners, and our expressions, and our ages, and our experience, even I can hardly believe that I am looking at three other myselves. No layman would entertain for a moment the notion that he beheld four versions of the same woman.

Did I say a moment? Not for an age of moments, particularly if the layman were indeed *a man.*

"Janet, may I ask you why you and your neighbors do not show up on our instruments? You must have discovered the theory of probability travel some time ago (in your terms), yet you are the first traveler. You wish to visit other universes of probability, yet you make it impossible for anyone to find you, let alone visit you.

"Why is that?"

"Aggressive and bellicose persons," said Janet with care, "always assume that unaggressive and pacific persons cannot protect themselves.

"Why is that?"

VI

Over trays of pre-cooked steak and chicken that would've disgraced an airline (that's where they came from, I found out later) Jael sat next to Jeannine and glued herself to Jeannine's ear, glancing round at the rest of us from time to time to see how we were taking it. Her eyes sparkled with the gaiety of corruption, the Devil in the fable tempting the young girl. Whisper, whisper, whisper. All I could hear were the sibilants, when her tongue came between her teeth. Jeannine stared soberly ahead and didn't eat much, the color leaving her little by little. Jael didn't eat at all. Like a vampire she fed on Jeannine's ear. Later she drank a sort of super-bouillon which nobody else could stand and talked a lot to all of us about the war. Finally, Janet said bluntly:

"What war?"

"Does it matter?" said Miss Reasoner ironically, raising her silver eyebrows. "This war, that war, isn't there always one?"

"No," said Janet.

"Well, hell," said Jael more genuinely, *"the* war. If there isn't one, there just was one, and if there wasn't

163

one, there soon will be one. Eh? The war between Us and Them. We're playing it rather cool just now because it's hard to work up an enthusiasm for something forty years old."

I said, "Us and Them?"

"I'll tell you," said Sweet Alice, making a face. "After the plague—don't worry; everything you eat is stuffed with anti-toxins and we'll decontaminate you before you go—besides, this all ended more than seventy years ago—after the bacteriological weapons were cleaned out of the biosphere (insofar as that was possible) and half the population buried (the dead half, I hope) people became rather conservative. They tend to do that, you know. Then after a while you get the reaction against the conservatism, I mean the radicalism. And after that the reaction against the radicalism. People had already begun gathering in like-minded communities before the war: Traditionalists, Neo-Feudalists, Patriarchalists, Matriarchalists, Separatists (all of us now), Fecundists, Sterilists, and what-have-you. They seemed to be happier that way. The War Between the Nations had really been a rather nice war, as wars go; it wiped the have-not nations off the face of the earth and made their resources available to us without the bother of their populations; all our machinery was left standing; we were getting wealthier and wealthier. So if you were not one of the fifty percent who had died, you were having a pretty good time of it. There was increasing separatism, increasing irritability, increasing radicalism; then came the Polarization; then came the Split. The middle drops out and you're left with the two ends, hein? So when people began shopping for a new war, which they also seem to do, don't they, there was only one war left. The only war that makes any sense if you except the relations between children and adults, which you must do because children grow up. But in the other war the Haves never stop being Haves and the Have-nots never stop being Have-nots. It's cooled off now, unfortunately, but no wonder; it's been going on for forty years—a stalemate, if you'll forgive the pun. But in my opinion, questions that are based on something real ought to be settled by something real without all this damned lazy miserable drifting. I'm a fanatic. I want to see this thing settled. I want to see it over and done with. Gone. Dead.

"Oh, don't worry!" she added. "Nothing spectacular is going to happen. All I will do in three days or so is ask you about the tourist trade in your lovely homes. What's wrong with that? Simple, eh?

"But it will get things moving. The long war will start up again. We will be in the middle of it and I—who have always been in the middle of it—will get some decent support from my people at last."

"Who?" said Jeannine crossly. "Who, who, for Heaven's sake! Who's Us, who's Them? Do you expect us to find out by telepathy!"

"I beg your pardon," said Alice Reasoner softly. "I thought you knew. I had no intention of puzzling you. You are my guests. When I say Them and Us I mean of course the Haves and the Have-nots, the two sides, there are always two sides, aren't there?

"I mean the men and the women."

Later I caught Jeannine by the door as we were all leaving; "What did she talk to you about?" I said. Something had gotten into Jeannine's clear, suffering gaze; something had muddied her timidity. What can render Miss Dadier self-possessed? What can make her so quietly stubborn? Jeannine said:

"She asked me if I had ever killed anybody."

VII

She took us topside in the branch elevator: The Young One, The Weak One, The Strong One, as she called us in her own mind. I'm the author and I know. *Miss Sweden* (she also called Janet this) ran her hands over the paneling and studied the controls while the other two gaped. Think of me in my usual portable form. Their underground cities are mazes of corridors like sunken hotels; we passed doors, barricades, store windows, branch corridors leading to arcades. What is this passion for living underground? At one barrier they put us in purdah, that is, some kind of asbestos-like fireman's suit that protects you against other people's germs and them against yours. But this time it was a fake, meant only to hide us. "Can't have them looking at you," said Jael. She went apart with the border guard and there was some low-voiced, aggressive byplay, some snarling and lifting of hackles which a third party resolved by a kind of rough joking. I didn't hear a word of it. She told us honestly that we couldn't be expected to believe anything we hadn't seen with our own eyes. There would be no films, no demonstrations, no statistics, unless we asked for them. We trundled out of the elevator into an armored car waiting in a barn, and across an unpaved, shell-pocked plain, a sort of no-man's-land, in the middle of the night. *Is the grass growing? Is that a virus blight? Are the mutated strains taking over?* Nothing but gravel, boulders, space, and stars. Jael flashed her pass at a second set of guards and told them about us, jerking her thumb backwards at the three of us: unclean, unclean, unclean. No barriers, no barbed wire, no searchlights; only the women have these. Only the men make a sport of people-hunting across the desert. Bulkier than three pregnancies, we followed our creatrix into another car, from out that first one, through the rubble and ruin at the edges of an old city, left standing just as it had been during the plague. Teachers come out here on Sundays, with their classes. It looks as if it's been used for target practice, with holes in everything and new scars, like mortar scars, on the rubble.

"It has," says Jael Reasoner. Each of us wears a luminous, shocking-pink cross on chest and back to show how deadly we are. So the Manlanders (who all carry guns) won't take pot-shots at us. There are lights in the distance—don't think I know any of this by hearsay; I'm the spirit of the author and know all things. I'll know it when we begin to pass the lit-up barracks at the edge of the city, when we see in the distance the homes of the very rich shining from the seven hilltops on which the city is built; I'll know it when we go through a tunnel of rubble, built fashionably to resemble a World War I trench, and emerge neither into a public nursery (they're either much further inside the city proper or out in the country) nor into a brothel, but into a recreation center called The Trench or The Prick or The Crotch or The Knife. I haven't decided on a name yet. The Manlanders keep their children with them only when they're very rich—but what posit I? Manlanders have no children. Manlanders buy infants from the Womanlanders and bring them up in batches, save for the rich few who can order children made from their very own semen: keep them in city nurseries until they're five, then out into the country training ground, with the gasping little misfits buried in baby cemeteries along the way. There, in ascetic and healthful settlements in the country, little boys are made into Men—though · some don't quite make it; sex-change surgery begins at sixteen. One out of seven fails early and makes the full change; one out of seven fails later and (refusing surgery) makes only half a change: artists, illusionists, impressionists of femininity who keep their genitalia but who grow slim, grow languid, grow emotional and feminine, all this the effect of spirit only. Five out of seven Manlanders make it; these are "real-men." The others are "the changed" or "the half-changed." All real-men like the changed; some real-men like the half-changed; none of the real-men like real-men, for that would be abnormal. Nobody asks the changed or half-changed what *they* like. Jael flashed her civil pass at the uniformed real-man at the entrance to The Crotch and we trundled after. Our hands and feet look very small to me, our bodies odd and dumpy.

We went inside; "Jael!" I exclaimed, "there are—"

"Look again," she said.

Look at the necks, look at the wrists and ankles, penetrate the veils of false hair and false eyelashes to measure the relative size of eyes and bone structure. The half-changed starve themselves to be slim, but look at their calves and the straightness of their arms and knees. If most of the fully changed live in harims and whore-homes, and if popular slang is beginning to call

167

them "cunts," what does this leave for us? What can we be called?

"The enemy," said Jael. "Sit here." We sat around a large table in the corner where the light was dim, snuggling up to the fake oak paneling. One of the guards, who had followed us inside, came up to Jael and put one giant arm round her, one huge paw crushing her bearishly to his side, his crimson epaulets, his gold boots, his shaved head, his sky-blue codpiece, his diamond-chequered-costumed attempt to beat up the whole world, to shove his prick up the world's ass. She looked so plain next to him. She was all swallowed up.

"Hey, hey," he said. "So you're back again!"

"Well, sure, why not?" (she said) "I have to meet someone. I have some business to do."

"Business!" he said fetchingly. "Don't you want some of the real thing? Come on, fuck business!"

She smiled gracefully but remained modestly silent. This seemed to please him. He enveloped her further, to the point of vanishment, and said in a low voice with a sort of chuckle:

"Don't you dream about it? Don't all you girls dream about us?"

"You know that, Lenny," she said.

"Sure I do," he said enthusiastically. "Sure. I can see it in your face whenever you come here. You get excited just looking at it. Like the doctors say, we can do it with each other but you can't because you don't have nothing to do it with, do you? So you don't get any."

"Lenny—" she began (slipping under his arm) "you got us figured out just right. Scout's honor. I've got business to do."

"Come on!" he said (pleading, I think).

"Oh, you're a brick!" cried Jael, moving behind the table, "you surely are. Why, you're so strong, some day you're going to squash us to death." He laughed, basso-profundo. "We're friends," he said, and winked laboriously.

"Sure," said Jael dryly.

"Some day you're gonna walk right in here—" and this tiresome creature began all over again, but whether he noticed the rest of us or saw someone or smelt someone I don't know, for suddenly he lumbered off in a great hurry, rousting his billy-club out of his azure sash, next the gun holster. Bouncers don't use their guns at The Prick; too much chance of hitting the wrong people. Jael was talking to someone else, a shadowy, thin-lipped party in a green, engineer's suit.

"Of course we're friends," said Jael Reasoner patiently. "Of course we are. That's why I don't want to talk to you tonight. Hell, I don't want to get you in trouble. See those crosses? One jab, one little rip or tear, and those girls will start an epidemic you won't be able to stop for a month. Do you want to be mixed up in that? Now you know we women are into plague research; well, these are some of the experiments. I'm taking them across Manland to another part of our own place; it's a short-cut. I wouldn't take them through here except I have some business to do here tonight. We're developing a faster immunization process. I'd tell all your friends to stay away from this table, too, if I were you—not that we can't take care of ourselves and *I* don't worry; I'm immune to this particular strain—but I don't want to see you take the rap for it. You've done a lot for me in the past and I'm grateful. I'm very grateful. You'd get it in the neck, you know. And you might get plague, too, there's always that. Okay?"

Astonishing how each of them has to be reassured of my loyalty! says Jael Reasoner. Even more astonishing that they believe me. They're not very bright, are they? But these are the little fish. Besides, they've been separated from real women so long that they don't know what to make of us; I doubt if even the sex surgeons know what a real woman looks like. The specifications we send them every year grow wilder and wilder and there isn't a murmur of protest. I think they like it. As moths to the flame, so men to the social patterns of the Army, that womanless world haunted by the ghosts of millions of dead women, that discarnate femininity that hovers over everybody and can turn the toughest real-man into one of Them, that dark force they always feel at the backs of their own minds! Would I, do you think, force slavishness and deformity

169

on two-sevenths of my own kind? Of course not! I think these men are not human. No, no, that's wrong—I decided long ago that they weren't human. Work is power, but they farm out everything to us without the slightest protest—Hell, they get lazier and lazier. They let us do their thinking for them. They even let us do their feeling for them. They are riddled with duality and the fear of duality. And the fear of themselves. I think it's in their blood. What human being would—sweating with fear and rage—mark out two equally revolting paths and insist that her fellow-creatures tread one or the other?

Ah, the rivalries of cosmic he-men and the worlds they must conquer and the terrors they must face and the rivals they must challenge and overcome!

"You are being a little obvious," says Janet pedantically from inside her suit, "and I doubt that the power of the blood—"

Hsst! Here comes my contact.

Our contact was a half-changed, for Manlanders believe that child care is woman's business; so they delegate to the changed and the half-changed the business of haggling for babies and taking care of children during those all-important, first five years—they want to fix their babies' sexual preferences early. This means, practically speaking, that the children are raised in brothels. Now some Manlander real-men do not like the idea of the whole business being in the hands of the feminized and the effeminate but there's not much they can do about it (see Proposition One, about child care, above)—although the more masculine look forward to a time when no Manlander will fall away from the ranks of the he-men, and with an obstinacy I consider perverse, refuse to decide who will be the sexual objects when the changed and the half-changed are no more. Perhaps they think sex beneath them. Or above them? (Around the shrine of each gowned and sequinned hostess in The Knife are at least three real-men; how many can a hostess take on in one night?) I suspect we real women still figure, however grotesquely, in Manland's deepest dreams; perhaps on that morning of Total Masculinity they will all invade Womanland, rape everyone

170

in sight (if they still remember how) and then kill them, and after that commit suicide upon a pyramid of their victims' panties. The official ideology has it that women are poor substitutes for the changed. I certainly hope so. (Little girls, crept out of their crèche at last, touching those heroic dead with curious, wee fingers. Nudging them with their patent leather Mary Janes. Bringing their baby brothers out to a party on the green, all flutes and oats and pastoral fun until the food gives out and the tiny heroines must decide: Whom shall we eat? The waving limbs of our starfish siblings, our dead mothers, or those strange, huge, hairy bodies already beginning to swell in the sun?) I flashed that damned pass—again!—this time at a half-changed in a pink chiffon gown, with gloves up to his shoulder, a monument of irrelevancy on high heels, a pretty girl with too much of the right curves and a bobbing, springing, pink feather boa. Where oh where is the shop that makes those long rhinestone earrings, objects of fetishism and nostalgia, worn only by the half-changed (and usually not by them unless they're rich), hand-made from museum copies, of no use or interest to fully six-sevenths of the adult human race? Somewhere stones are put together by antiquarians, somewhere petroleum is transformed into fabric that can't burn without polluting the air, and won't rot, and won't erode, so that strands of plastic have turned up in the bodies of diatoms at the bottom of the Pacific Trench—such a vision was he, so much he wore, such folds and frills and ribbons and buttons and feathers, trimmed like a Christmas tree. Like Garbo playing Anna Karenina, decorated all over. His green eyes shrewdly narrowed. This one has intelligence. Or is it only the weight of his false lashes? The burden of having always to be taken, of having to swoon, to fall, to endure, to hope, to suffer, to wait, to only be? There must be a secret feminine underground that teaches them how to behave; in the face of their comrades' derision and savage contempt, in the face of the prospect of gang rape if they're found alone on the streets after curfew, in the face of the legal necessity to belong—every one of them—to a real-man, somehow they still

171

learn the classic shiver, the slow blink, the knuckle-to-lip pathos. These, too, I think, must be in the blood. But whose? My three friends and I pale beside such magnificence! Four lumpy parcels, of no interest to anyone at all, at all.

Anna, with a mechanical shiver of desire, says that we must go with him.

"Her?" says Jeannine, confused.

"Him!" says Anna in a strained contralto. The half-changed are very punctilious—sometimes about the changeds' superiority and sometimes about their own genitals. Either way it works out to *Him*. He's extraordinarily aware, for a man, of Jeannine's shrinking and he resents it—as who would not? I myself am respectful of ruined lives and forced choices. On the street once Anna did not fight hard enough against the fourteen-year-old toughs who wanted his twelve-year-old ass; he didn't go to the extremity of berserk rage, reckoning his life as nothing in defense of his virility; he forestalled—by surrender—the plucking out of an eye, the castration, the throat cut with a broken bottle, the being put out of his twelve-year-old action with a stone or a tire chain. I know a lot about Manlanders' history. Anna made a *modus vivendi*, he decided life was worth it on any terms. Everything follows from that.

"Oh, you're lovely," says Jeannine, heartfelt. Sisters in misfortune. This really pleases Anna. He shows us a letter of safe-conduct he has from his boss—a realman, of course—and putting it back in his pink-brocaded evening bag, draws around him that fake-feather Thing which floats and wobbles in the least current of air. It's a warm evening. To protect his employé, the big boss (they are Men, even in the child-rearing business) has had to give Anna K a little two-way TV camera to wear in his ear; otherwise somebody would break his high heels and leave him dead or half-dead in an alley. Everybody knows that the half-changed are weak and can't protect themselves; what do you think femininity is all about? Even so Anna probably has a bodyguard waiting at the entrance to The Knife. I'm cynical enough to wonder sometimes if the Manlanders' mystique isn't just an excuse to feminize anybody with a pretty face—but look again, they believe it; look under the padding, the paint, the false hair, the corsetry, the skin rinses and the magnificent dresses and you'll see nothing exceptional, only faces and bodies like any other man's. Anna bats his eyes at us and wets his lips, taking the women inside the suits to be real-men, taking me to be a real-man (what else can I be if I'm not a changed?), taking the big wide world itself to be—what else?—a Real-Man intent on worshipping Anna's ass; the world exists to look at Anna; he—or she—is only a real-man turned inside out.

An eerie sisterliness, a smile at Jeannine. All that narcissism! Brains underneath, though.

Remember where their loyalties lie.

(Are they jealous of us? I don't think they believe we're women.)

He wets his lips again, the indescribable silliness of that insane mechanism, practiced anywhere and everywhere, on the right people, on the wrong people. But what else is there? It seems that Anna's boss wants to meet me. (I don't like that.) But we'll go; we maintain our outward obedience until the very end, until the beautiful, bloody moment that we fire these stranglers, these murderers, these unnatural and atavistic nature's bastards, off the face of the earth.

"Dearest sister," says Anna softly, sweetly, "come with me."

VIII

I guess Anna's boss just wanted to see the alien poontang. I don't know yet what he wants, but I will. His wife clicked in with a tray of drinks—scarlet skintights, no underwear, transparent high-heeled sandals like Cinderella's—she gave us a homey, cute smile (she wears no make-up and is covered with freckles) and stilted out. Man talk. They seldom earn wives before fifty. Art, they say, has had a Renaissance among the Manlander rich, but this one doesn't look like a patron:

173

jowly, pot-bellied, the fierce redness of an athlete forced into idleness. His heart? High blood pressure? But they all cultivate their muscles and let their health and their minds rot. There is a rather peculiar wholesomeness to the home life of a Manland millionaire; Boss, for example, would not think of letting his wife go anywhere alone—that is, risk the anarchy of the streets—even with a bodyguard. He knows what's due her. Their "women," they say, civilize them. For an emotional relationship, turn to a "woman."

What am I?

I know what I am, but what's my brand name?

He stares rudely, unable to conceal it: *What are they? What do they do? Do they screw each other? What does it feel like?* (Try and tell him!) He doesn't waste a second on the pink crosses in purdah; they're only "women" anyhow (he thinks); *I'm* the soldier, *I'm* the enemy, *I'm* the other self, the mirror, the masterslave, the rebel, the heretic, the mystery that must be found out at all costs. (Maybe he thinks the three J's have leprosy.) I don't like this at all. J-one (Janet, by her gait) is examining the paintings on the wall; J-two and J-three stand hand in hand, Babes in the Wood. Boss finishes his drink, chewing on something in the bottom of it like a large teddy-bear, with comic deliberation: chomp, chomp. He waves grandly toward the other drinks, his wife having abandoned the tray on top of what looks for all the world like a New Orleans, white-enamelled, bordello piano (Whorehouse Baroque is very big in Manland right now).

I shook my head.

He said, "You have any children?" Pregnancy fascinates them. The rank-and-file have forgotten about menstruation; if they remembered, *that* would fascinate them. I shook my head again.

His face darkened.

"I thought," said I mildly, "that we were going to talk business. I'd like to do just that. I don't mean—that is, I don't want to be unsociable, but time's passing and I'd rather not discuss my personal life."

He said: "You're on my turf, you'll Goddamn well talk about what I Goddamn well talk about."

174

Let it pass. Control yourself. Hand them the victory in the Domination Sweepstakes and they usually forget whatever it is they were going to do anyway. He glared and brooded. Munched chips, crackers, saltsticks, what-not. Doesn't really know what he wants. I waited.

"Personal life!" he muttered.

"It's not really very interesting," I volunteered.

"You kids screw each other?"

I said nothing.

He leaned forward. "Don't get me wrong. I think you have a right to do it. I never bought this stuff about women alone having no sex. It's not in human nature. Now, do you?"

"No," I said.

He chuckled. "That's right, cover up. Mind, I'm not condemning you. It's only to be expected. Eh! If we'd kept together, men and women, none of this would have happened. Right?"

I put on my doubtful, slightly shamed, sly, well-you-know, all-purpose look. I have never known what it means, but they seem to. He laughed out loud. Another drink.

"Look here," he said, "I expect you have more intelligence than most of those bitches or you wouldn't be in this job. Right? Now it's obvious to anyone that we need each other. Even in separate camps we still have to trade, you still have to have the babies, things haven't changed that much. Now what I have in mind is an experimental project, a pilot project, you might say, in trying to get the two sides back together. Not all at once—"

"I—" I said. (They don't hear you.)

"Not all at once," (he continued, deaf as a post) "but a little bit at a time. We have to make haste deliberately. Right?"

I was silent. He leaned back. "I knew you'd see it," he said. Then he made a personal remark: "You saw my wife?" I nodded.

"Natalie's grand," he said, taking some more chips. "She's a grand girl. She made these. Deep-fried,

175

I think." (A weak woman handling a pot of boiling oil.) "Have some."

To pacify him I took some and held them in my hand. Greasy stuff.

"Now," he said, "you like the idea, right?"

"What?"

"The aversive therapy, for Chrissakes, the pilot group. Social relations, getting back together. I'm not like some of the mossbacks around here, you know, I don't go for this inferior-superior business; I believe in equality. If we get back together, it has to be on that basis. Equals."

"But——" I said, meaning no offense.

"It has to be on the basis of equality! I believe that. And don't think the man in the street can't be sold on it, propaganda to the contrary. We're brought up on this nonsense of woman's place and woman's nature when we don't even have women around to study. What do we know! I'm not any less masculine because I've done woman's work; does it take less intelligence to handle an operation like the nurseries and training camps than it does to figure the logistics of War Games? Hell, no! Not if you do it rationally and efficiently; business is business."

Let it go. Perhaps it'll play itself out; they do sometimes. I sat attentively still while he gave me the most moving plea for my own efficiency, my rationality, my status as a human being. He ended by saying anxiously, "Do you think it'll work?"

"Well——" I began.

"Of course, of course," (interrupted this damned fool once again) "you're not a diplomat, but we have to work through the men we have, don't we? Individual man can accomplish ends where Mass-man fails. Eh?"

I nodded, picturing myself as Individual Man. The "woman's work" explains it, of course; it makes him dangerously irritable. He had gotten now into the poignant part, the mystifying and moving account of our Sufferings. This is where the tears come in. It helps to be able to classify what they're going to do, but Lord! it's depressing, all the same. Always the same. I

176

sit on, perfectly invisible, a chalk sketch of a woman. An idea. A walking ear.

"What we want" (he said, getting into stride) "is a world in which everybody can be *himself*. Him. Self. Not this insane forcing of temperaments. Freedom. Freedom for all. I admire you. Yes, let me say that I do indeed, and most frankly, admire you. You've broken through all that. Of course most women will not be able to do that—in fact, most women—given the choice—will hardly choose to give up domesticity altogether or even" (here he smiled) "even choose to spend much of their lives in the market-place or the factory. Most women will continue to choose the conservative caretaking of childhood, the formation of beautiful human relationships, and the care and service of others. Servants. Of. The. Race. Why should we sneer at that? And if we find there are certain traits connected with sex, like homemaking, like reasoning power, like certain temperamental factors, well of course there will be, but why derogate one sex or the other on that account? People" (braced for the peroration) "people are as they are. If—"

I rose to my feet. "Excuse me," I said, "but business—"

"Damn your business!" he said in heat, this confused and irritable man. "Your business isn't worth two cents compared with what I'm talking about!"

"Of course not, of course not," I said soothingly.

"I should hope so!"

Numb, numb. With boredom. Invisible. Chained.

"That's the trouble with you women, you can't see anything in the abstract!"

He wants me to cringe. I really think so. Not the content of what I say but the endless, endless feeding of his vanity, the shaky structure of self. Even the intelligent ones.

"Don't you appreciate what I'm trying to do for you?"

Kiss-me-I'm-a-goodguy.

"Don't you have any idea how important this is?"

Sliding down the slippery gulf into invisibility.

"This could make history!"

177

Even me, with all my training!

"Of course, we have a tradition to uphold."

It'll be slow.

"—we'll have to go slowly. One thing at a time."

If it's practical.

"We'll have to find out what's practicable. This may be—uh—visionary. It may be in advance of its time."

Can't legislate morality.

"We can't force people against their inclinations and we have generations of conditioning to overcome. Perhaps in a decade—"

Perhaps never.

"—perhaps never. But men of good will—"

Did he hear that?

"—and women, too, of course, you understand that the word 'men' includes the word 'women'; it's only usage—"

Everyone must have his own abortion.

"—and not really important. You might even say" (he giggles) " 'everyone and his husband' or 'everyone will be entitled to his own abortion' " (he roars) "but I want you to go back to your people and tell them—"

It's unofficial.

"—that we're prepared to negotiate. But it can't be official. You must understand that I face considerable opposition. And most women—not, you, of course; you're different—well, most women aren't used to thinking a thing *through* like this. They can't do it systematically. Say, you don't mind my saying that about 'most women,' do you?"

I smile, drained of personality.

"That's right," (he said) "don't take it personally. Don't get feminine on me," and he winked broadly to show he bore me no ill-will. This is the time for me to steal away, leaving behind half my life's blood and promises, promises, promises; but you know what? I just can't do it. It's happened too often. I have no reserves left. I sat down, smiling brilliantly in sheer anticipation, and the dear man hitched his chair nearer. He looks uneasy and avid. "We're friends?" he says.

"Sure," I say, hardly able to speak.

178

"Good!" he said. "Tell me, do you like my place?"

"Oh yes," I say.

"Ever see anything like it before?"

"Oh no!" (I live in a chicken-barn and eat shit.)

He laughed delightedly. "The paintings are pretty good. We're having a kind of Renaissance lately. How's art among the ladies, huh?"

"So-so," I said, making a face. The room is beginning to sway with the adrenalin I can pump into my bloodstream when I choose; this is called voluntary hysterical strength and it is very, very useful, yes indeed. First the friendly chat, then the uncontrollably curious grab, and then the hatred comes out. Be prepared.

"I suppose," he said, "you must've been different from the start—from a little girl, eh?—doing a job like this. You've got to admit we have one thing up on you—we don't try to force everybody into the same role. Oh no. We don't keep a man out of the kitchen if that's what he really wants."

"Oh sure," I said. (Those chemical-surgical castrati.)

"Now you do," he said. "You're more reactionary than we are. You won't *let* women lead the domestic life. You want to make everyone alike. That's not what I visualize."

He goes into a long happy rap about motherhood, the joys of the uterus. The emotional nature of Woman. The room is beginning to sway. One gets very reckless in hysterical strength; the first few weeks I trained, I broke several of my own bones but I know how to do it now. I really do. My muscles are not for harming anyone else; they are to keep me from harming myself. That terrible concentration. That feverish brightness. Boss-Idiot has not talked to anyone else about his grand idea; he's still in First Cliché stage and any group discussion, however moronic, would have weeded out the worst of them. His dear Natalie. His gifted wife. Take me, now; he loves me. Yes he does. Not physically, of course. Oh no. Life seeks its mate. Its complement. Romantic rubbish. Its other self. Its

179

joy. He won't talk business tonight. Will he ask me to stay over?

"Oh, I couldn't," says the other Jael. He doesn't hear it; there's a gadget in Boss's ear that screens out female voices. He's moved closer, bringing his chair with him—some silly flub-dub about not being able to talk the length of the room. Spiritual intimacy. Smiling foolishly he says:

"So you like me a little, huh?"

How terrible, betrayal by lust. No, ignorance. No—pride.

"Hell, go away," I say.

"Sure you do!" He expects me to act like his Natalie, he bought her, he owns her. What do women do in the daytime? What do they do when they're alone? Adrenalin is a demanding high; it untunes all your finer controls.

"Get away," I whisper. He doesn't hear it. These men play games, play with vanity, hiss, threaten, erect their neck-spines. It sometimes takes ten minutes to get a fight going. I, who am not a reptile but only an assassin, only a murderess, never give warning. They worry about *playing fair,* about *keeping the rules,* about *giving a good acount of themselves.* I don't play. I have no pride. I don't hesitate. At home I am harmless, but not here.

"Kiss me, you dear little bitch," he says in an excited voice, mastery and disgust warring with each other in his eyes. Boss has never seen a real cunt, I mean as nature made them. He'll use words he hasn't dared to use since he was eighteen and took his first half-changed in the street, mastery and disgust mingling. That slavish apprenticeship at the recreation centers. How can you love anyone who is a castrated You? Real homosexuality would blow Manland to pieces.

"Take your filthy hands off me," I say clearly, enjoying his enjoyment of my enjoyment of his enjoyment of that cliché. Has he forgotten the three lepers?

"Send them away," he mutters in agony, "send them away! Natalie can do them," forgetting gender in his haste. Or perhaps he really thinks they are my lov-

180

ers. Women will do what men find too disgusting, too difficult, too demeaning.

"Look," I say, grinning uncontrollably, "I want to be perfectly clear. I don't want your revolting lovemaking. I'm here to do business and relay any reasonable message to my superiors. I'm not here to play games. *Cut it out.*"

But when do they ever listen!

"You're a woman," he cries, shutting his eyes, "you're a beautiful woman. You've got a hole down there. You're a beautiful woman. You've got real, round tits and you've got a beautiful ass. You want me. It doesn't matter what you say. You're a woman, aren't you? This is the crown of your life. This is what God made you for. I'm going to fuck you. I'm going to screw you until you can't stand up. You want it. You want to be mastered. Natalie wants to be mastered. All you women, you're all women, you're sirens, you're beautiful, you're waiting for me, waiting for a man, waiting for me to stick it in, waiting for me, me, me."

Et patati et patata; the mode is a wee bit over-familiar. I told him to open his eyes, that I didn't want to kill him with his eyes shut, for God's sake.

He didn't hear me.

"OPEN YOUR EYES!" I roared, "BEFORE I KILL YOU!" and Boss-man did.

He said, *You led me on.*

He said, *You are a prude.* (He was shocked.)

He said, *You deceived me.*

He said, *You are a Bad Lady.*

This we can cure!—as they say about pneumonia. I think the J's will have sense enough to stay out of it. Boss was muttering something angry about his erection so, angry enough for two, I produced my own—by this I mean that the grafted muscles on my fingers and hands pulled back the loose skin, with that characteristic, itchy tickling, and of course you are wise; you have guessed that I do not have Cancer on my fingers but Claws, talons like a cat's but bigger, a little more dull than wood brads but good for tearing. And my teeth are a sham over metal. Why are men so afraid of the awful intimacies of hate? Remember, I don't threaten. I

181

don't play. I always carry firearms. The truly violent are never without them. I could have drilled him between the eyes, but if I do that, I all but leave my signature on him; it's freakier and funnier to make it look as if a wolf did it. Better to think his Puli went mad and attacked him. I raked him gaily on the neck and chin and when he embraced me in rage, sank my claws into his back. You have to build up the fingers surgically so they'll take the strain. A certain squeamishness prevents me from using my teeth in front of witnesses—the best way to silence an enemy is to bite out his larynx. Forgive me! I dug the hardened cuticle into his neck but he sprang away; he tried a kick but I wasn't there (I told you they rely too much on their strength); he got hold of my arm but I broke the hold and spun him off, adding with my nifty, weighted shoon another bruise on his limping kidneys. Ha ha! He fell on me (you don't feel injuries, in my state) and I reached around and scored him under the ear, letting him spray urgently into the rug; he will stagger to his feet and fall, he will plunge fountainy to the ground; at her feet he bowed, he fell, he lay down; at her feet he bowed, he fell, he lay down dead.

Jael. Clean and satisfied from head to foot. Boss is pumping his life out into the carpet. All very quiet, oddly enough. Three J's in a terrible state, to judge from their huddling together; I can't read their hidden faces. Will Natalie come in? Will she faint? Will she say, "I'm glad to be rid of him, the old bastard?" Who will own her now? You get monomaniacal on adrenalin. "Come on, come on!" I whispered to the J's, herding them toward the door, buzzing and humming, the stuff still singing in my blood. The stupidity of it. The asininity of it. I love it, I love it. "Come on!" I said. Pushing them out the door, into the corridor, out and into the elevator, past the fish swimming in the aquatic wall, evil, svelte manta-rays and groupers six feet long. Poor fish! No business done today, God damn, but once they get that way there's no doing business with them; you have to kill them anyway, might as well have fun. There's no standing those non-humans at all, at all. Jeannie is calm. Joanna is ashamed of me. Janet is weeping. But how do you expect me to stand for this all month? How do you expect me to stand it all year? Week after week? For twenty years? Little male voice says: It Was Her Menstrual Period. Perfect explanation! Raging hormonal imbalances. His ghostly voice: "You did it because you had your period. Bad girl." Oh beware of unclean vessels who have that dir-ty menstrual period and Who Will Not Play! I shooed the J's into the Boss-man's car—Anna had long ago disappeared—skeleton keys out of my invisible suit with its invisible pocket, opened the lock, fired the car, started up. I'll go on Automatic as soon as we get to the highway; Boss's I.D. will carry us to the border. No trouble from there.

"You all right?" I asked the J's, laughing, laughing, laughing. I'm drunk still. They said Yes in varying musical keys. The Strong One's voice is pitched higher than that of The Weak One (who believes she's an alto), and The Little One is highest of all. Yes, yes, they said, frightened. Yes, yes, yes.

"Now I did not get that contract signed," I said, putting on my sham teeth over my steel ones. "God damn, God damn, God damn!" (Don't drive on adrenalin; you'll probably have an accident.)

"When does it leave you?" That's The Strong One: smart girl. "An hour, half an hour," I said. "When we get home."

"Home?" (from the back)

"Yes. My home." Every time I do this I burn up a little life. I shorten my time. I'm at the effusive stage now, so I bit my lip, to keep quiet.

After a long silence—"Was that necessary?" from The Weak One.

Still hurt, still able to be hurt by them! Amazing. You'd think my skin would get thicker, but it doesn't. We're all of us still flat on our backs. The boot's on our neck while we slowly, ever so slowly, gather the power and the money and the resources into our own hands. While they play war games. I put the car on Autom. and sat back, chilly with the reaction. My heartbeat's quieting. Breath slower.

Was it necessary? (Nobody says this.) You could

have turned him off—maybe. You could have sat there all night. You could have nodded and adored him until dawn. You could have let him throw his temper tantrum; you could have lain under him—what difference does it make to you?—you'd have forgotten it by morning.

You might even have made the poor man happy.

There is a pretense on my own side that we are too refined to care, too compassionate for revenge—this is bullshit, I tell the idealists. "Being with Men," they say, "has changed you."

Eating it year in and year out.

"Look, was it necessary?" says one of the J's, addressing to me the serious urgency of womankind's eternal quest for love, the ages-long effort to heal the wounds of the sick soul, the infinite, caring compassion of the female saint.

An over-familiar mode! Dawn comes up over the waste land, bringing into existence the boulders and pebbles battered long ago by bombs, dawn gilding with its pale possibilities even the Crazy Womb, the Ball-breaking Bitch, the Fanged Killer Lady.

"I don't give a damn whether it was necessary or not," I said.

"I liked it."

IX

It takes four hours to cross the Atlantic, three to shuttle to a different latitude. Waking up in a Vermont autumn morning, inside the glass cab, while all around us the maples and sugar maples wheel slowly out of the fog. Only this part of the world can produce such color. We whispered at a walking pace through wet fires. Electric vehicles are quiet, too; we heard the drip of water from the leaves. When the house saw us, my old round lollipop-on-a-stick, it lit up from floor to top, and as we came nearer broadcast the Second Brandenburg through the black, wet tree-trunks and the fiery

184

leaves, a delicate attention I allow myself and my guests from time to time. Shouting brilliantly through the wet woods—I prefer the unearthly purity of the electronic scoring. One approaches the house from the side, where it looks almost flat on its central column—only a little convex, really—it doesn't squat down for you on chicken legs like Baba Yaga's hut, but lets down from above a great, coiling, metal-mesh road like a tongue (or so it seems; in reality it's only a winding staircase). Inside you find yourself a corridor away from the main room; no use wasting heat.

Davy was there. The most beautiful man in the world. Our approach had given him time to make drinks for us—which the J's took from his tray, staring at him but he wasn't embarrassed—curled up most un-waiterlike at my feet with his hands around his knees and proceeded to laugh at the right places in the con-versation (he takes his cues from my face).

The main room is panelled in yellow wood with a carpet you can sleep on (brown) and a long, glassed-in porch from which we watch the blizzards sweep by five months out of the year. I like purely visual weather. It's warm enough for Davy to go around naked most of the time, my ice lad in a cloud of gold hair and nudity, never so much a part of my home as when he sits on the rug with his back against a russet or vermilion chair (we mimic autumn here), his drowned blue eyes fixed on the winter sunset outside, his hair turned to ash, the muscles of his back and thighs stirring a little. The house hangs oddments from the ceiling; found objects, mobiles, can openers, red balls, bunches of wild grass, and Davy plays with them.

I showed the J's around: the books, the microfilm viewer in the library in touch with our regional library miles away, the storage spaces in the walls, the various staircases, the bathrooms molded of glass fiber and put together from two pieces, the mattresses stored in the walls of the guest rooms, and the conservatory (near the central core, to make use of the heat) where Davy comes and mimics wonder, watching the lights shine on my orchids, my palmettos, my bougainvillea, my whole little mess of tropical plants. I even have a glassed-in

space for cacti. There are outside plantings where in
season you can find mountain laurel, a tangled maze of
rhododendron, scattered irises that look like an expensive and antique cross between insects and lingerie—
but these are under snow now. I even have an electri-
fied fence, inherited from my predecessor, that encloses
the whole estate to keep out the deer and occasionally
kills trees which take the mild climate around the house
a little too much for granted.

I let the J's peep into the kitchen, which is an
armchair with controls like a 707's, but not the place
where I store my tools and from which I have access to
the central core when House has indigestion. That's
dirty and you need to know what you're doing. I
showed them Screen, which keeps me in touch with my
neighbors, the nearest of whom is ten miles away, Telephone, who is my long-distance backup line, and Phonograph, where I store my music.

Jeannine said she didn't like her drink; it wasn't
sweet enough. So I had Davy dial her another.

Do you want dinner? (She blushed.)

My palace and gardens (said I) I acquired late in
life when I became rich and influential; before that I
lived in one of the underground cities among the
damnedest passel of neighbors you ever saw, sentimental
Arcadian communes—underground, mind you!—
whose voices would travel up the sewer pipes at all the
wrong times of day and night, shrill sacrifices to love
and joy when you want to sleep, ostentatious shudder-
ing whenever I appeared in the corridor, wincing and
dashing back inside to huddle together like kittens, conscious of their own innocence, and raise their pure
young voices in the blessedness of community song.
You know the kind: "But we were having *fun!*" in a
soft, wondering, highly reproachful voice while she
closes the door gently but firmly on your thumb. They
thought I was Ultimate Evil. They let me know it.
They are the kind who want to win the men over by
Love. There's a game called Pussycat that's great fun
for the player; it goes like this: Meeow, I'm dead (lying
on your back, all four paws engagingly held in the air,
playing helpless); there's another called Saint George

186

and the Dragon with You Know Who playing You
Know What; and when you can no longer tolerate either, you do as I did: come home in a hobgoblin-head
of a disguise, howling and chasing your neighbors
down the hall while they scream in genuine terror
(well, sort of).

Then I moved.

That was my first job, impersonating one of the
Manlanders' police (for ten minutes). By "job" I don't
mean what I was sent to do last night, that was open
and legitimate, but a "job" is a little bit under the table.
It took me years to throw off the last of my Pussy-fet-
ters, to stop being (however brutalized) vestigially
Pussy-cat-ified, but at last I did and now I am the rosy,
wholesome, single-minded assassin you see before you
today.

I come and go as I please. I do only what I want.
I have wrestled myself through to an independence of
mind that has ended by bringing all of you here today.
In short, I am a grown woman.

I was an old-fashioned girl, born forty-two years
ago in the last years before the war, in one of the few
mixed towns still left. It amazes me sometimes to think
of what my life would have been like without the war,
but I ended up in a refugee camp with my mother.
Maddened Lesbians did not put cigarette butts out on
her breasts, propaganda to the contrary; in fact she got
a lot more self-confident and whacked me when I tore
to pieces (out of pure curiosity) a paper doily that decorated the top of the communal radio—this departure
from previous practice secretly gratified me and I decided I rather liked the place. We were re-settled and I
was sent to school once the war cooled off; by '52 our
territories had shrunk to pretty much what they are today, and we've grown too wise since to think we can
gain anything by merely annexing land. I was trained
for years—we deplore what we must nonetheless
use!—and began my slow drift away from the community, that specialization (they say) that brings you
closer to the apes, though I don't see how such an ex-
ceedingly skilled and artificial practice can be anything
but quintessentially human.

187

At twelve I artlessly told one of my teachers that I was very glad I was being brought up to be a man-woman, and that I looked down on those girls who were only brought up to be woman-women. I'll never forget her face. She did not thrash me but let an older girl-girl do it—I told you I was old-fashioned. Gradually this sort of thing wears off; not everything with claws and teeth is a Pussycat. On the contrary!

My first job (as I told you) was impersonating one of the Manlander police; my most recent one was taking the place of a Manlander diplomat for eighteen months in a primitive patriarchy on an alternate Earth. Oh yes, the Men also have probability-travel, or rather they have it through us; we run the routine operations for them. So far has corruption progressed! With my silver hair, my silver eyes, and my skin artificially darkened to make me look even stranger to the savages, I was presented as a Prince of Faery, and in that character I lived in a dank stone castle with ghastly sanitary arrangements and worse beds for a year and a half. A place that would make your hair stand on end. Jeannine must stop looking so skeptical—please reflect that some societies stylize their adult roles to such a degree that a giraffe could pass for a man, especially with seventyseven layers of clothes on, and a barbarian prudery that keeps you from ever taking them off. They were impossible people. I used to make up stories about the Faery women; once I killed a man because he said something obscene about the Faery women. Think of that! You must imagine me as the quiet, serene Christian among the pagans, the courteous magician among the blunt men-o'-war, the overcivilized stranger (possibly a Demon because he was understood to have no beard) who spoke softly and never accepted challenges, but who was not afraid of anything under Heaven and who had a grip of steel. And so on. Oh, those cold baths! And the endless joking about how *they* weren't queer, by God! And the bellicosity, the continual joshing that catches in your skin like thorns and exasperates you almost to murder, and the constant fingering of sex and womankind with its tragic, pitiable bafflement and its even worse bragging; and last of all the perpetual losing battle with fear, the constant unloading of anxious weaknesses on to others (and their consequent enraged fury) as if fear and weakness were not the best guides we human beings ever had! Oh, it was rich! When they found that not a knight in the Men's House could lay a hand on me, they begged for instruction; I had half the warriors of the mead-hall doing elementary ballet under the mistaken impression that they were learning ju-jitsu. They may be doing it still. It made them sweat enough and it's my signature, plain as day, to the whole bloody universe and any Manlander who turns up there again.

A barbarian woman fell in love with me. It's terrible to see that slavishness in someone else's eyes, feel that halo she puts around you, and know from your own person the nature of that eager deference men so often perceive as admiration. *Validate me!* she cried. *Justify me! Raise me up! Save me from the others!* ("I am his wife," she says, turning the mystic ring round and round on her finger, "I am *his* wife.") So somewhere I have a kind of widow. I used to talk to her sensibly, as no man ever had before, I think. I tried to take her back with me, but couldn't get authorization for her. Somewhere out there is a murderess as rosy and single-minded as I, if we could only get to her.

May She save us all!

I saved the King's life once by pinning to the festive Kingly board a pretty little hamadryad somebody had imported from the Southern lands to kill His Majesty. This helped me a good deal. Those primitive warriors are brave men—that is, they are slaves to the fear of fear—but there are some things they believe every man is entitled to run from in abject terror, *viz.* snakes, ghosts, earthquakes, disease, demons, magic, childbirth, menstruation, witches, afreets, incubi, succubi, solar eclipses, reading, writing, good manners, syllogistic reasoning, and what we might generally call the less reliable phenomena of life. The fact that I was not afraid to pin a poisonous snake to a wooden table with a fork (a piece of Faery handicraft I had brought with me to eat meat with) raised my prestige immensely. Oh yes, if it had bitten me, I would have been dead. But they don't

189

move that fast. Think of me in quilting and crinolines—not like a Victorian lady, like a player in Kabuki—holding up that poor little broken-backed dinkus amid general hurrahs. Think of me astride a coal-black charger, my black-and-silver cloak streaming in the wind under a heraldic banner comprising crossed forks on a field of reptile eggs. Think of anything you please. Think, if you will, how hard it is to remain calm under constant insults, and of the genuine charm of playing bullfight with a big, beautiful, nasty blond who goes hartyhar every chance he gets, and whom you can reel in and spin out again as if you knew all his control buttons, as indeed you do. Think of giving the King bad advice week after week: modestly, deliberately, and successfully. Think of placing your ladylike foot on the large, dead neck of a human dinosaur who has bothered you for months and has finally tried to kill you; there he lies, this big, carnal flower gathered at last by Chaos and Old Night, torn and broken in the dust, a big limpid Nada, a nothing, a thing, an animal, a creature brought down at last out of his pride to the truth of his organic being—*and you did it.*

I keep one precious souvenir of that time: the look on the face of my most loyal feudal retainer when I revealed my sex to him. This was a man I had all-but-seduced without his knowing it—little touches on the arm, the shoulder, the knee, a quiet manner, a certain look in the eyes—nothing so gross that he thought it to be in me; he assumed it was all in himself. I loved that part. His first impulse, of course, was to hate me, fight me, drive me off—but I wasn't doing anything, was I? I had made no advances to him, had I? What sort of mind did he have? A pitiable confusion! So I got even nicer. He got madder and guiltier, of course, and loathed the very sight of me because I made him doubt his own reason; finally he challenged me and I turned him into a faithful dog by beating him right into the ground; I kicked that man so bloody hard that I couldn't stand it myself and had to explain to him that what he believed were unnatural lusts were really a species of religious reverence; he just wanted to lie peacefully on the ground and kiss my boot.

The day that I left I went out into the hills with a few friends for the Faery "ceremony" that was to take me away, and when the Bureau people radio'd me they were ready, I sent the others away, and I told him the truth. I divested myself of my knightly attire (no mean trick, considering what those idiots wear) and showed him the marks of Eve; for a moment I could see that stinking bastard's whole world crumble. For a moment he *knew*. Then, by God, his eyes got even more moist and slavish, he sank to his knees and piously elevating his gaze, exclaimed in a rapture of feudal enthusiasm—Humanity mending its fences—

If the women of Faery are like this, just think what the MEN must be!

One of Her little jokes. Oh Lord, one of Her hardest jokes.

If you want to be an assassin, remember that you must decline all challenges. Showing off is not your job.

If you are insulted, smile meekly. Don't break your cover.

Be afraid. This is information about the world.

You are valuable. Push yourself.

Take the easiest way out whenever possible. Resist curiosity, pride; and the temptation to defy limits. You are not your own woman and must be built to last.

Indulge hatred. Action comes from the heart.

Pray often. How else can you quarrel with God?

Does this strike you as painfully austere? If not, you are like me; you can turn yourself inside out, you can live for days upside down, the most biddable, unblushing servant of the Lady since the Huns sacked Rome, just for fun. Anything pursued to its logical end is revelation; as Blake says, The path of Excess leads to the Palace of Wisdom, to that place where all things converge but up high, up unbearably high, that mental success which leads you into yourself, under the aspect of eternity, where you are limber and nice, where you act eternally under the aspect of Everything and where—by doing the One Genuine Thing—you cannot do anything untruly or half-way.

To put it simply: those are the times that I am most myself.

Sometimes I am a little remorseful; I grow sorry that the exercise of my art entails such unpleasant consequences for other people, but really! Hate is a material like any other. If you want me to do something else useful, you had better show me what that something else is. Sometimes I go into one of our cities and have little sprees in the local museums; I look at pictures, I get a hotel room and take long hot baths, I drink lots of lemonade. But the record of my life is the record of work, slow, steady, responsible work. I tied my first sparring partner in enraged knots, as Brynhild tied up her husband in her girdle and hung him on the wall, but aside from that I have never hurt a fellow Womanlander; when I wanted to practice deadly strategies, I did it on the school robot. Nor do I have love-affairs with other women; in some things, as I told you, I am a very old-fashioned girl.

The art, you see, is really in the head, however you train the body.

What does all this mean? That I am your hostess, your friend, your ally. That we are in the same boat. That I am the grand-daughter of Madam Cause; my great-aunts are Mistress Doasyouwouldbedoneby and her slower sister, Mistress Bedonebyasyoudid. As for my mother, she was an ordinary woman—that is to say, very helpless—and as my father was pure appearance (and hence nothing at all), we needn't trouble about him.

Everything I do, I do *by Cause,* that is to say *Because,* that is to say out of necessity, will-I, nill-I, ineluctably, because of the *geas* laid on me by my grandmother Causality.

And now—since hysterical strength affects me the way staying up all night affects you—I'm going to sleep.

X

In my sleep I had a dream and this dream was a dream of guilt. It was not human guilt but the kind of helpless, hopeless despair that would be felt by a small

192

wooden box or geometrical cube if such objects had consciousness; it was the guilt of sheer existence.

It was the secret guilt of disease, of failure, of ugliness (much worse things than murder); it was an attribute of my being like the greenness of the grass. It was *in* me. It was *on* me. If it had been the result of anything I had done, I would have been less guilty.

In my dream I was eleven years old.

Now in my eleven years of conventional life I had learned many things and one of them was what it means to be convicted of rape—I do not mean the man who did it, I mean the woman to whom it was done. Rape is one of the Christian mysteries, it creates a luminous and beautiful tableau in people's minds; and as I listened furtively to what nobody would allow me to hear straight out, I slowly came to understand that I was face to face with one of those shadowy feminine disasters, like pregnancy, like disease, like weakness; she was not only the victim of the act but in some strange way its perpetrator; somehow she had attracted the lightning that struck her out of a clear sky. A diabolical chance—*which was not chance*—had revealed her to all of us as she truly was, in her secret inadequacy, in that wretched guiltiness which she had kept hidden for seventeen years but which now finally manifested itself in front of everybody. Her secret guilt was this:

She was Cunt.

She had "lost" something.

Now the other party to the incident had manifested his essential nature, too; he was Prick—but being Prick is not a bad thing. In fact, he had "gotten away with" something (possibly what she had "lost").

And there I was, listening at eleven years of age:

She was out late at night.

She was in the wrong part of town.

Her skirt was too short and that provoked him.

She liked having her eye blacked and her head banged against the sidewalk.

I understood this perfectly. (I reflected thus in my dream, in my state of being a pair of eyes in a small wooden box stuck forever on a gray, geometric

193

plane—or so I thought.) I too had been guilty of what
had been done to me, when I came home from the
playground in tears because I had been beaten up by
bigger children who were bullies.

I was dirty.

I was crying.

I demanded comfort.

I was being inconvenient.

I did not disappear into thin air.

And if that isn't guilt, what is? I was very lucid in
my nightmare. I knew it was not wrong to be a girl because Mommy said so; cunts were all right if they were
neutralized, one by one, by being hooked on to a man,
but this orthodox arrangement only partly redeems
them and every biological possessor of one knows in
her bones that radical inferiority which is only another
name for Original Sin.

Pregnancy, for example (says the box), take pregnancy now, it's a disaster, but we're too enlightened to
blame the woman for her perfectly natural behavior,
aren't we? Only keep it secret and keep it going—and
I'll give you three guesses as to which partner the pregnancy is in.

When you grow up as an old-fashioned girl, you
always remember that cozy comfort: Daddy getting angry a lot but Mummy just sighs. When Daddy says,
"For God's sake, can't you women ever remember anything without being told?" he isn't asking a real question any more than he'd ask a real question of a lamp
or a wastebasket. I blinked my silver eyes inside my
box. If you stumble over a lamp and you curse that
lamp and then you become aware that inside that lamp
(or that wooden box or that pretty girl or that piece of
bric-a-brac) is a pair of eyes watching you *and that pair
of eyes is not amused*—what then?

Mommy never shouted, "I hate your bloody
guts!" She controlled herself to avoid a scene. That was
her job.

I've been doing it for her ever since.

Now here the idiot reader is likely to hit upon a
fascinating speculation (maybe a little late), that my
guilt is blood-guilt for having killed so many men. I

suppose there is nothing to be done about this. Anybody who believes I feel guilty for the murders I did is a Damned Fool in the full Biblical sense of those two words; you might as well kill yourself right now and save me the trouble, especially if you're male. I am not guilty because I murdered.

I murdered because I was guilty.

Murder is my one way out.

For every drop of blood shed there is restitution made; with every truthful reflection in the eyes of a dying man I get back a little of my soul; with every gasp of horrified comprehension I come a little more into the light. See? It's *me!*

I am the force that is ripping out your guts; I, I, I, the hatred twisting your arm; I, I, I, the fury who has just put a bullet into your side. It is I who cause this pain, not you. It is I who am doing it to you, not you. It is I who will be alive tomorrow, not you. Do you know? Can you guess? Are you catching on? It is I, whom you will not admit exists.

Look! Do you *see me?*

I, I, I. Repeat it like magic. That is not me. I am not that. Luther crying out in the choir like one possessed: NON SUM, NON SUM, NON SUM!

This is the underside of my world.

Of course you don't want me to be stupid, bless you! you only want to make sure you're intelligent. You don't want me to commit suicide; you only want me to be gratefully aware of my dependency. You don't want me to despise myself; you only want to ensure the flattering deference to you that you consider a spontaneous tribute to your natural qualities. You don't want me to lose my soul; you only want what everybody wants, things to go your way; you want a devoted helpmeet, a self-sacrificing mother, a hot chick, a darling daughter, women to look at, women to laugh at, women to come to for comfort, women to wash your floors and buy your groceries and cook your food and keep your children out of your hair, to work when you need the money and stay home when you don't, women to be enemies when you want a good fight, women who are sexy when you want a good lay, women who don't

195

complain, women who don't nag or push, women who don't hate you really, women who know their job, and above all—women who lose. On top of it all, you sincerely require me to be happy; you are naively puzzled that I should be so wretched and so full of venom in this best of all possible worlds. Whatever can be the matter with me? But the mode is more than a little outworn.

As my mother once said: The boys throw stones at the frogs in jest.

But the frogs die in earnest.

XI

I don't like didactic nightmares. They make me sweat. It takes me fifteen minutes to stop being a wooden box with a soul and to come back to myself in ordinary human bondage.

Davy sleeps nearby. You've heard about blue-eyed blonds, haven't you? I passed into his room barefoot and watched him curled in sleep, unconscious, the golden veils of his eyelashes shadowing his cheeks, one arm thrown out into the streak of light falling on him from the hall. It takes a lot to wake him (you can almost mount Davy in his sleep) but I was too shaken to start right away and only squatted down by the mattress he sleeps on, tracing with my fingertips the patterns the hair made on his chest: broad high up, over the muscles, then narrowing toward his delicate belly (which rose and fell with his breathing), the line of hair to below the navel, and then that suddenly stiff blossoming of the pubic hair in which his relaxed genitals nestled gently, like a rosebud.

I told you I was an old-fashioned girl.

I caressed his dry, velvety-skinned organ until it stirred in my hand, then ran my fingernails lightly down his sides to wake him up; I did the same—though very lightly—to the insides of his arms.

He opened his eyes and smiled starrily at me.

196

It's very pleasant to follow Davy's hairline around his neck with your tongue or nuzzle all the hollows of his long-muscled, swimmer's body: inside the elbows, the forearms, the place where the back tapers inward under the ribs, the backs of the knees. A naked man is a cross, the juncture elaborated in vulnerable and delicate flesh like the blossom on a banana tree, that place that's given me so much pleasure.

I nudged him gently and he shivered a little, bringing his legs together and spreading his arms flat; with my forefinger I made a transient white line on his neck. Little Davy was half-filled by now, which is a sign that Davy wants to be knelt over. I obliged, sitting across his thighs, and bending over him without touching his body, kissed him again and again on the mouth, the neck, the face, the shoulders. He is very, very exciting. He's very beautiful, my classic mesomorphic monster-pet. Putting one arm under his shoulders to lift him up, I rubbed my nipples over his mouth, first one and then the other, which is nice for us both, and as he held on to my upper arms and let his head fall back, I pulled him to me, kneading his back muscles, kneading his buttocks, sliding down to the mattress with him. Little Davy is entirely filled out now.

So lovely: Davy with his head thrown to one side, eyes closed, his strong fingers clenching and unclenching. He began to arch his back, as his sleepiness made him a little too quick for me, so I pressed Small Davy between thumb and forefinger just enough to slow him down and then—when I felt like it—playfully started to mount him, rubbing the tip of him, nipping him a little on the neck. His breathing in my ear, fingers convulsively closing on mine.

I played with him a little more, tantalizing him, then swallowed him whole like a watermelon seed—so fine inside! with Davy moaning, his tongue inside my mouth, his blue gaze shattered, his whole body uncontrollably arched, all his sensation concentrated in the place where I held him.

I don't do this often, but that time I made him come by slipping a finger up his anus: convulsions, fires, crying in no words as the sensation was pulled out of him. If I had let him take more time, I would have climaxed with him, but he's stiff for quite a while after he comes and I prefer that; I like the after-tremors and the after-hardness, slipperier and more pliable than before; Davy has an eerie malleability at those times. I grasped him internally, I pressed down on him, enjoying in the one act his muscular throat, the hair under his arms, his knees, the strength of his back and buttocks, his beautiful face, the fine skin on the inside of his thighs. Kneaded and bruised him, hiccoughing inside with all my architecture: little buried rod, swollen lips and grabby sphincter, the flexing half-moon under the pubic bone. And everything else in the vicinity, no doubt. I'd had him. Davy was mine. Sprawled blissfully over him—I was discharged down to my fingertips but still quietly throbbing—it had really been a good one. His body so warm and wet under me and inside me.

XII

And looked up to see—

XIII

—the three J's—

XIV

"Good Lord! Is *that* all?" said Janet to Joanna.

XV

Something pierces the sweetest solitude.

I got up, tickled him with the edge of my claw, joined them at the door. Closing it. "Stay, Davy." This is one of the key words that the house "understands"; the central computer will transmit a pattern of signals to the implants in his brain and he will stretch out obediently on his mattress; when I say to the main computer "Sleep," Davy will sleep. You have already seen what else happens. He's a lovely limb of the house. The original germ-plasm was chimpanzee, I think, but none of the behavior is organically controlled any more. True, he does have his minimal actions which he pursues without me—he eats, eliminates, sleeps, and climbs in and out of his exercise box—but even these are caused by a standing computer pattern. And I take precedence, of course. It is theoretically possible that Davy has (tucked away in some nook of his cerebrum) consciousness of a kind that may never even touch his active life—is Davy a poet in his own peculiar way?—but I prefer to believe not. His consciousness—such as it is and I am willing to grant it for the sake of argument—is nothing but the permanent possibility of sensation, a mere intellectual abstraction, a nothing, a picturesque collocation of words. It is experientially quite empty, and above all, it is nothing that need concern you and me. Davy's soul lies somewhere else; it's an outside soul. Davy's soul is in Davy's beauty; and Beauty is always empty, always on the outside. Isn't it?

"Leucotomized," I said (to the J's). "Lobotomized. Kidnapped in childhood. Do you believe me?"

They did.

"Don't," I said. Jeannine doesn't understand what we're talking about; Joanna does and is appalled; Janet is thinking. I shooed them into the main room and told them who he was.

Alas! those who were shocked at my making love that way to a man are now shocked at my making love to a machine; you can't win.

"Well?" said the Swedish Miss.

"Well," said I, "this is what we want. We want bases on your worlds; we want raw materials if you've got them. We want places to recuperate and places to hide an army; we want places to store our machines. Above all, we want places to move from—bases that the other side doesn't know about. Janet is obviously acting as an unofficial ambassador, so I can talk to her, that's fine. You two might object that you are persons of no standing, but whom do you expect me to ask, your governments? Also, we need someone who can show us the local ropes. You'll do fine for me. You are the authorities, as far as I'm concerned.

"Well?

"Is it yes or no?

"Do we do business?"

PART NINE

I

This is the Book of Joanna.

II

I was driving on a four-lane highway in North America with an acquaintance and his nine-year-old son.

"Beat 'im! Beat 'im!" cried the little boy excitedly as I passed another car in order to change lanes. I stayed in the right-hand lane for a while, admiring the buttercups by the side of the road, and then, in order to change lanes back, fell behind another car.

"Pass 'im! Pass 'im!" cried the distressed child, and then in anxious tears, "Why didn't you *beat* 'im?"

"There, there, old sport," said his indulgent Daddy, "Joanna drives like a lady. When you're grown up you'll have a car of your own and you can pass everybody on the road." He turned to me and complained:

"Joanna, you just don't drive aggressively enough."

In training.

III

There's the burden of knowledge. There's the burden of compassion. There's seeing all too clearly what's in their eyes as they seize your hands, crying cheerily, "You don't really mind my saying that, do you? I knew you didn't!" Men's shaky egos have a terrible appeal to the mater dolorosa. At times I am seized by a hopeless, helpless longing for love and reconciliation, a dreadful yearning to be understood, a teary passion for exposing our weaknesses to each other. It seems intolerable that I should go through life thus estranged, keeping it all to my guilty self. So I try to explain in the softest, least accusing way I can, but oddly enough men don't behave the way they do on the Late Late Show, I mean those great male stars in their infancy in the Jean Arthur or the Mae West movies: candid, clear-eyed, and fresh, with their unashamed delight in their women's strength and their naive enjoyment of their own, beautiful men with beautiful faces and the joyfulness of innocents, John Smith or John Doe. These are the only men I will let into Whileaway. But we have fallen away from our ancestors' softness and clarity of thought into corrupt and degenerate practices. When I speak now I am told loftily or kindly that I just don't understand, that women are really happy that way, that women can better themselves if they want to but somehow they just don't want to, that I'm joking, that I can't possibly mean what I say, that I'm too intelligent to be put in the same class as "women," that I'm different, that there is a profound spiritual difference between men and women of which I don't appreciate the beauty, that I have a man's brain, that I have a man's mind, that I'm talking to a phonograph record. Women don't take it that way. If you bring up the subject with them, they begin to tremble out of terror, embarrassment, and alarm; they smile a smile of hideous, smug embarrassment, a magical smile meant to wipe them off the face of the earth, to make them abject and invisible—oh no, no, no, no, don't think I believe any of that, don't think I need any of that! Consider:

You *ought to be interested in* politics.

Politics is baseball. Politics is football. Politics is X "winning" and Y "losing." Men wrangle about politics in living rooms the way Opera Fan One shouts at Opera Fan Two about Victoria de los Angeles.

No squabble between the Republican League and the Democrat League will ever change *your* life. Concealing your anxiety over the phone when He calls; that's your politics.

Still, you *ought to be interested in* politics. Why aren't you?

Because of feminine incapacity.

One can go on.

IV

I committed my first revolutionary act yesterday. I shut the door on a man's thumb. I did it for no reason at all and I didn't warn him; I just slammed the door shut in a rapture of hatred and imagined the bone breaking and the edges grinding into his skin. He ran downstairs and the phone rang wildly for an hour after while I sat, listening to it, my heart beating wildly, thinking wild thoughts. Horrible. Horrible and wild. I must find Jael.

Women are so petty (translation: we operate on too small a scale).

Now I'm worse than that—I also do not give a damn about humanity or society. It's very upsetting to think that women make up only one-tenth of society, but it's true. For example:

My doctor is male.

My lawyer is male.

My tax-accountant is male.

The grocery-store-owner (on the corner) is male.

The janitor in my apartment building is male.

The president of my bank is male.

The manager of the neighborhood supermarket is male.

My landlord is male.
Most taxi-drivers are male.
All cops are male.
All firemen are male.
The designers of my car are male.
The factory workers who made the car are male.
The dealer I bought it from is male.
Almost all my colleagues are male.
My employer is male.
The Army is male.
The Navy is male.
The government is (mostly) male.
I think most of the people in the world are male.

Now it's true that waitresses, elementary-school teachers, secretaries, nurses, and nuns are female, but how many nuns do you meet in the course of the usual business day? Right? And secretaries are female only until they get married, at which time, they change or something because you usually don't see them again at all. I think it's a legend that half the population of the world is female; where on earth are they keeping them all? No, if you tot up all those categories of women above, you can see clearly and beyond the shadow of a doubt that there are maybe 1–2 women for every 11 or so men and that hardly justifies making such a big fuss. It's just that I'm selfish. My friend Kate says that most of the women are put into female-banks when they grow up and that's why you don't see them, but I can't believe that.

(Besides, what about the children? Mothers have to sacrifice themselves to their children, both male and female, so that the children will be happy when they grow up; though the mothers themselves were once children and were sacrificed to in order that they might grow up and sacrifice themselves to others; and when the daughters grow up, *they* will be mothers and *they* will have to sacrifice themselves for *their* children, so you begin to wonder whether the whole thing isn't a plot to make the world safe for (male) children. But motherhood is sacred and mustn't be talked about.)

Oh dear, oh dear.
Thus in the bad days, in the dark swampy times.

At thirteen desperately watching TV, curling my long legs under me, desperately reading books, callow adolescent that I was, trying (desperately!) to find someone in books, in movies, in life, in history, to tell me it was O.K. to be ambitious, O.K. to be loud, O.K. to be Humphrey Bogart (smart and rudeness), O.K. to be James Bond (arrogance), O.K. to be Superman (power), O.K. to be Douglas Fairbanks (swashbuckling), to tell me self-love was all right, to tell me I could love God and Art and Myself better than anything on earth and still have orgasms.

Being told it was all right "for you, dear," but not for *women.*

Being told I was a woman.

At sixteen, giving up.

In college, educated women (I found out) were frigid; active women (I knew) were neurotic; women (we all knew) were timid, incapable, dependent, nurturing, passive, intuitive, emotional, unintelligent, obedient, and beautiful. You can always get dressed up and go to a party. Woman is the gateway to another world; Woman is the earth-mother; Woman is the eternal siren; Woman is purity; Woman is carnality; Woman has intuition; Woman is the life-force; Woman is selfless love.

"I am the gateway to another world," (said I, looking in the mirror) "I am the earth-mother; I am the eternal siren; I am purity," (Jeez, new pimples) "I am carnality; I have intuition; I am the life-force; I am selfless love." (Somehow it sounds different in the first person, doesn't it?)

Honey (said the mirror, scandalized) Are you out of your fuckin' *mind?*

I AM HONEY
I AM RASPBERRY JAM
I AM A VERY GOOD LAY
I AM A GOOD DATE
I AM A GOOD WIFE
I AM GOING CRAZY

Everything was preaches and cream.

(When I decided that the key word in all this vomit was *self-less* and that if I was really all the things

205

books, friends, parents, teachers, dates, movies, relatives, doctors, newspapers, and magazines said I was, then if I acted as I pleased without thinking of all these things I would be all these things in spite of my not trying to be all these things. So—

(*"Christ, will you quit acting like a man!"*)

Alas, it was never meant for us to hear. It was never meant for us to know. We ought never be taught to read. We fight through the constant male refractoriness of our surroundings; our souls are torn out of us with such shock that there isn't even any blood. Remember: I didn't and don't want to be a "feminine" version or a diluted version or a special version or a subsidiary version or an ancillary version, or an adapted version of the heroes I admire. I want to be the heroes themselves.

What future is there for a female child who aspires to being Humphrey Bogart?

Baby Laura Rose, playing with her toes, she's a real pretty little sweetie-girl, isn't she?

> Sugar and spice
> And everything nice—
> *That's* what little girls are made of!

But her brother's a tough little bruiser (two identical damp, warm lumps). At three and a half I mixed sour cream and ice cubes on the window sill to see if they would turn into *ice cream;* I copied the words "hot" and "cold" off the water faucets. At four I sat on a record to see if it would break if pressure were applied evenly to both sides—it did; in kindergarten I taught everybody games and bossed them around; at six I beat up a little boy who took candy from my coat; I thought very well of myself.

206

V

Learning to
despise
one's
self

VI

Brynhild hung her husband on a nail in the wall,
tied up in her girdle as in a shopping bag, but she, too,
lost her strength when the magic shlong got inside her.
One can't help feeling that the story has been somewhat
distorted in the re-telling. When I was five I thought
that the world was a matriarchy.

I was a happy little girl.

I couldn't tell the difference between "gold" and
"silver" or "night gown" and "evening gown," so I
imagined all the ladies of the neighborhood getting together in their beautiful "night gowns"—which were
signs of rank—and making all the decisions about our
lives. They were the government. My mother was President because she was a school teacher and local people
deferred to her. Then the men would come home from
"work" (wherever that was; I thought it was like hunt-
ing) and lay "the bacon" at the ladies' feet, to do with
as they wished. The men were employed by the ladies
to do this. Laura Rose, who never swam underwater a
whole month in summer camp with goggles on or slept
in the top bunk, fancying herself a Queen in lonely
splendor or a cabin-boy on a ship, has no such happy
memories. She's the girl who wanted to be Genghis
Khan. When Laura tried to find out who she was, they
told her she was "different" and that's a hell of a de-
scription on which to base your life; it comes down to

207

either "Not-me" or "Convenient-for me" and what is one supposed to do with that? What am I to do? (she says) What am I to feel? Is "supposed" like "spoused"? Is "different" like "deteriorate"? How can I eat or sleep? How can I go to the moon?

I first met Laur a few years ago when I was already grown up. Cinnamon and apples, ginger and vanilla, that's Laur. Now having Brynhildic fantasies about her was nothing—I have all sorts of extraordinary fantasies which I don't take seriously—but bringing my fantasies into the real world frightened me very much. It's not that they were bad in themselves, but they were Unreal and therefore culpable; to try to make Real what was Unreal was to mistake the very nature of things; it was a sin not against conscience (which remained genuinely indifferent during the whole affair) but against Reality, and of the two the latter is far more blasphemous. It's the crime of creating one's own Reality, of "preferring oneself" as a good friend of mine says. I knew it was an impossible project.

She was reading a book, her hair falling over her face. She was radiant with health and life, a study in dirty blue jeans. I knelt down by her chair and kissed her on the back of her smooth, honeyed, hot neck with a despairing feeling that *now I had done it*—but asking isn't getting. Wanting isn't having. She'll refuse and the world will be itself again. I waited confidently for the rebuke, for the eternal order to reassert itself (as it had to, of course)—for it would in fact take a great deal of responsibility off my hands.

But she let me do it. She blushed and pretended not to notice. I can't describe to you how reality itself tore wide open at that moment. She kept on reading and I trod at a snail's pace over her ear and cheek down to the corner of her mouth, Laur getting hotter and redder all the time as if she had steam inside her. It's like falling off a cliff, standing astonished in mid-air as the horizon rushes away from you. If this is possible, anything is possible. Later we got stoned and made awkward, self-conscious love, but nothing that happened afterward was as important to me (in an unhuman way) as that first, awful wrench of the mind.

Once I felt the pressure of her hip-bone along my belly, and being very muddled and high, thought: *She's got an erection.* Dreadful. Dreadful embarrassment. One of us had to be male and it certainly wasn't me. Now they'll tell me it's because I'm a Lesbian, I mean that's why I'm dissatisfied with things. That's not true. It's not because I'm a Lesbian. It's because I'm a *tall, blonde, blue-eyed Lesbian.*

Does it count if it's your best friend? Does it count if it's her mind you love through her body? Does it count if you love men's bodies but hate men's minds? Does it count if you still love yourself?

Later we got better.

VII

Jeannine goes window-shopping. She has my eyes, my hands, my silly stoop; she's wearing my blue plastic raincoat and carrying my umbrella. Jeannine is out on the town on a Saturday afternoon saying goodbye, goodbye, goodbye to all that.

Goodbye to mannequins in store windows who pretend to be sympathetic but who are really nasty conspiracies, goodbye to hating Mother, goodbye to the Divine Psychiatrist, goodbye to The Girls, goodbye to Normality, goodbye to Getting Married, goodbye to The Supernaturally Blessed Event, goodbye to being Some Body, goodbye to waiting for Him (poor fellow!), goodbye to sitting by the telephone, goodbye to feebleness, goodbye to adoration, goodbye Politics, hello politics. She's scared but that's all right. The streets are full of women and this awes her; where have they all come from? Where are they going? (If you don't mind the symbolism.) It's stopped raining but mist coils up from the pavement. She passes a bridal shop where the chief mannequin, a Vision in white lace and tulle, sticks out her tongue at Jeannine. "Didn't do it!" cries the mannequin, resuming her haughty pose and balancing a bridal veil on her head. Jeannine shuts her umbrella, latches it, and swings it energetically round and round.

Goodbye. Goodbye. Goodbye to everything.

We met in Schrafft's and sat, the four of us, at one table, ordering their Thanksgiving dinner, argh, which is so traditional you can't stand it. Gah.

"What's Indian pudding?" says Janet, baffled.

"No, don't, better not," says Joanna.

We munch in silence, slowly, the way Whileaway-ans eat: munch, munch, gulp. Munch. Gulp, gulp, gulp, Munch. Meditatively. It's pleasant to eat. Janet screws up her eyes, yawns, and stretches athletically, leaning over the back of her chair and working her bent arms first to this side, then to that. She ends up by pounding on the table. "Mm!" she says.

"My goodness, look at that," says Jeannine, very self-possessed and elegant, her fork in mid-air. "I thought you were going to knock someone's hat off."

Schrafft's is full of women. Men don't like places like this where the secret maintenance work of femininity is carried on, just as they turn green and bolt when you tell them medical events are occurring in your gen-ito-urinary system. Jael has got something stuck between her steel teeth and her sham ones, and cocking an eye around Schrafft's, she slips off her tooth cover and roots around for the blackberry seed or whatever, exposing to the world her steely, crocodilian grin. Back they go. In. Done.

"So?" says Jael. "Do we do business?" There is a long, uncomfortable silence. I look around Schrafft's and wonder why women at their most genteel are so miserly; why is there no Four Seasons, no Maxim's, no Chambord, for women? Women are very strange about money, feudal almost: Real Money is what you spend on the house and on yourself (except for your appearance): Magic Money is what you get men to spend on you. It takes a tremendous rearrangement of mental priorities for women to eat well, that is to spend money on their insides instead of their outsides. The Schrafft's hostess stands by the cashier's desk in her good black dress and sensible shoes; women left to themselves are ugly, *i.e.* human, but Gentility has been interfering here.

"This is awful food," says Janet, who is used to Whileaway.

"This is wonderful food," says Jael, who is used to Womanland and Manland.

Both burst out laughing.

"Well?" says Jael again. Another silence. Janet and I are very uncomfortable. Jeannine, one cheek bulging like a squirrel's, looks up as if surprised that we could hesitate to do business with Womanland. She nods briefly and then goes back to building mashed-sweet-potato mountains with her fork. Jeannine now gets up late, neglects the housework until it annoys her, and plays with her food.

"Jeannine?" says Jael.

"Oh, sure," says Jeannine, "*I* don't mind. You can bring in all the soldiers you want. You can take the whole place over; I wish you would." Jael goes admiringly tsk tsk and makes a rueful face that means: my friend, you are really going it. "My whole world calls me Jeannie," says Jeannine in her high, sweet voice. "See?"

(Laur is waiting outside for Janet, probably baring her teeth at passing men.)

To Janet, Jael suddenly says:

"You don't want me?"

"No," says Janet. "No, sorry."

Jael grins. She says:

"Disapprove all you like. Pedant! Let me give you something to carry away with you, friend: that 'plague' you talk of is a lie. *I know.* The world-lines around you are not so different from yours or mine or theirs and there is no plague in any of them, not any of them. Whileaway's plague is a big lie. Your ancestors lied about it. It is I who gave you your 'plague,' my dear, about which you can now pietize and moralize to your heart's content; I, I, I, I am the plague, Janet Evason. I and the war I fought built your world for you, I and those like me, we gave you a thousand years of peace and love and the Whileawayan flowers nourish themselves on the bones of the men we have slain."

211

"No," said Janet dryly, "I don't believe." Now you must know that Jeannine is Everywoman. I, though I am a bit quirky, I too am Everywoman. Every woman is not Jael, as Uncle George would say—but Jael is Everywoman. We all stared accusingly at Janet but Miss Evason was not moved. Laur came through Schrafft's revolving door and waved wildly; Janet got up to go.

"Think about it," said Alice Reasoner. "Go home and find out about it."

Janet began to weep—those strange, shameless, easy, Whileawayan tears that well out of the eyes without destroying the composed sadness of the face. She is expressing her grief about (for) Alice Reasoner. I think—when I stop to think about it, which is not often—that I like Jael the best of us all, that I would like to be Jael, twisted as she is on the rack of her own hard logic, triumphant in her extremity, the hateful hero with the broken heart, which is like being the clown with the broken heart. Jael averts her face in a death's-head grimace that is only a nervous tic of Alice Reasoner's, an expression that began perhaps twenty years ago as a tasting-something-sour look and has intensified with time into sheer bad-angelry, luminous with hate. She has cords in her neck. She could put out her captive's claws and slash Schrafft's tablecloth into ten separate, parallel ribbons. That's only one one-hundredth of what she can do. Jeannine is playing an absorbing game with her green peas (she had no dessert). Jeannine is happy.

We got up and paid our quintuple bill; then we went out into the street. I said goodbye and went off with Laur, I, Janet; I also watched them go, I, Joanna; moreover I went off to show Jael the city, I Jeannine, I Jael, I myself.

Goodbye, goodbye, goodbye.

Goodbye to Alice Reasoner, who says tragedy makes her sick, who says never give in but always go down fighting, who says take them with you, who says die if you must but loop your own intestines around the neck of your strangling enemy. Goodbye to everything. Goodbye to Janet, whom we don't believe in and whom we deride but who is in secret our savior from utter despair, who appears Heaven-high in our dreams with a mountain under each arm and the ocean in her pocket, Janet who comes from the place where the labia of sky and horizon kiss each other so that Whilea-wayans call it The Door and know that all legendary things come therefrom. Radiant as the day, the Might-be of our dreams, living as she does in a blessedness none of us will ever know, she is nonetheless Every-woman. Goodbye, Jeannine, goodbye, poor soul, poor girl, poor as-I-once-was. Goodbye, goodbye. Remem-ber: we will all be changed. In a moment, in the twin-kling of an eye, we will all be free. I swear it on my own head. I swear it on my ten fingers. We will be our-selves. Until then I am silent; I can no more. I am God's typewriter and the ribbon is typed out.

Go, little book, trot through Texas and Vermont and Alaska and Maryland and Washington and Florida and Canada and England and France; bob a curtsey at the shrines of Friedan, Millet, Greer, Firestone, and all the rest; behave yourself in people's living rooms, nei-ther looking ostentatious on the coffee table nor failing to persuade due to the dullness of your style; knock at the Christmas garland on my husband's door in New York City and tell him that I loved him truly and love him still (despite what anybody may think); and take your place bravely on the book racks of bus terminals and drugstores. Do not scream when you are ignored, for that will alarm people, and do not fume when you are heisted by persons who will not pay, rather rejoice that you have become so popular. Live merrily, little daughter-book, even if I can't and we can't; recite yourself to all who will listen; stay hopeful and wise. Wash your face and take your place without a fuss in the Library of Congress, for all books end up there eventually, both little and big. Do not complain when at last you become quaint and old-fashioned, when you grow as outworn as the crinolines of a generation ago and are classed with *Spicy Western Stories, Elsie Dins-more,* and *The Son of the Sheik;* do not mutter angrily to yourself when young persons read you to hrooch and hrch and guffaw, wondering what the dickens you were all about. Do not get glum when you are no longer understood, little book. Do not curse your fate. Do not reach up from readers' laps and punch the readers' noses.

Rejoice, little book!

For on that day, we will be free.